God on the Move is a readable, biblically based analytical masterpiece. It contains vital snippets from an array of proven missiologists and practitioners concerning the DMM paradigm of multiplication. The book highlights the basic features of DMM with amazing simplicity and practical field relevance drawn from globally acclaimed movements. It also includes convincingly clear responses to objections to the movement paradigm. This book will inspire and equip DMM trainers, practitioners, coaches, movement catalysts, missiologists, and theologians. It is a must-read for those passionate about bringing the fame of God's name to the least reached peoples of the world. I highly and heartily recommend it.

MIKE ADEGBILE
Movement Catalyst, Go-North Initiative
FCM Country Director for Nigeria, 24:14 Global Strategy Team

God on the Move is a field guide we've been waiting for—clear, compelling, and grounded in real movement leadership. I know and trust several of the contributors—Samuel Kebreab, Aila Tasse, Victor John—and their voices carry both spiritual weight and lived credibility. This book isn't just insightful, it's essential. If you care about multiplying disciples among the unreached, read this now. It will reshape how you pray, lead, and engage in God's global mission.

JOHN BECKER
Africa Inland Mission; Activate Global; 3P Ministries

Movements move; they tell a progressive story. Each link in a movement's chain reaction writes a new chapter of the Holy Spirit's work on the earth. The best way to understand why movements move is to listen to those who observe them. *God on the Move* helps you do that. Dave Coles has taken some of the best material in *Motus Dei* and made it more accessible—so those on a movement journey can get the benefit of those who have gone before.

HARRY BROWN
CEO, New Generations

Disciple making is the test of our evangelistic and church planting faithfulness. This book offers a hopeful critique of disciple-making models and offers wisdom grounded in Scripture, rooted in practical experience, and filled with amazing stories of conversion—of which God is the explanation. In this book, we have a picture of the "wheels" on which gospel breakthroughs are happening.

FRED DIMADO
Associate International Director, Pioneers

I am very thankful for the publication of *God on the Move*. It is written by some of the world's most outstanding disciple making practitioners, researchers, and scholars. I hope it is translated into many languages. It will inspire and provide insight to frontline workers and accelerate the multiplication of disciples, leaders, and churches around the world.

JIM EGLI, PhD
Curriculum Coordinator, New Generations

As an adjunct professor, missiologist, practitioner, and church-planting trainer, I wholeheartedly endorse *God on the Move*. This simplified edition of the groundbreaking *Motus Dei* work continues in the pioneering spirit that skillfully bridges academic depth with practical application. Given my passion for equipping leaders and exploring Disciple Making Movements, I am inspired by how this book integrates biblical principles, case studies, and methodologies to empower practitioners and leaders across diverse contexts. Don't bury this one on your bookshelf; it makes a great field application guide.

REV. MATT FRETWELL, DMin
Adjunct Professor, Regent University School of Divinity

I've recommended *Motus Dei* to more people than I can count. Its academic treatment of movements by reputable scholars and practitioners makes a unique contribution to movement literature. This simpler version, *God on the Move*, will be even easier to recommend. It will serve as an excellent guide for all readers—ranging from movement skeptics to those fully committed to movement approaches. The chapter on answering objections to CPM/DMM is incredibly valuable! I've referred to my copy of *Motus Dei* over and over again. I think you'll find yourself doing the same with this book!

CHRIS GALANOS
Pastor, Experience Life
Author, *From Megachurch to Multiplication*

This is a highly practical book, and the world needs more practical application of clear kingdom principles. It is filled with rare insights and applicable truths about church planting. The concepts have been tested on the ground and analyzed, making this an incredible resource for the body of Christ. I recommend you dive in and read it.

NEIL HART
Executive Head, Mergon Foundation
Author, *The Magnificent Exit*

God on the Move offers a compelling exploration into the essential rediscovery of the church as a dynamic movement rather than a static institution. Drawing on insights from leading thinkers and practitioners, this book is an indispensable resource for anyone seeking to lead transformative Jesus-centered movements in today's world.

ALAN HIRSCH
Founder, Movement Leaders Collective,
Forge Missional Training Network, and the 5Q Collective
Author of books on missional spirituality, leadership, and organization

During my forty-five years of involvement in church planting efforts among Muslims, the Holy Spirit has used my many mistakes to shift my focus—from a traditional gathered-church model to a dynamic movement of multiplying discipleship groups. However, I still had many questions—about how movements are structured, how leaders are developed, and how they relate to other churches. *Motus Dei* gave me many of the answers I was looking for, equipping me with greater understanding to be a better trainer and catalyst. I am delighted that *God on the Move* now makes these vital lessons accessible to a wider audience. I am sure it will result in a greater harvest for the glory of God.

JULYAN LIDSTONE
Church Planter and Trainer, Operation Mobilisation

When I read an advance copy of *God on the Move*, I instantly wished it was already published so I could start using it on the very same day. The case studies of real movements are both compelling and encouraging. The biblical backgrounds for movement thinking are convicting and motivating. The application of honesty and accountability in measuring and improving multiplication is, by itself, worth the price of admission. Taken as a whole, this book stands tall for both implementers and catalysts, as well as critics and naysayers. If you have an opinion about movements (either way), you need to read this book. I need to order a copy for each of the DMMers in our organization—seriously.

DOUG LUCAS, DBA
President, Team Expansion
Author, *More Disciples*, Editor, *Brigada*

Movements to Jesus from other religious backgrounds are not a fad—they are a fact. We are seeing this fact of history unfold before our very eyes. Those who refuse to see God's purposes through contextual lenses and are quick to critique these emergent movements merely reveal their ignorance of Scripture, history, and contemporary world Christianity. *God on the Move* presents a highly accessible introduction to movements today that represent millions of new Jesus-followers in some of the most hostile contexts around the world. I cannot recommend it highly enough. As you read, listen to the local leaders and global experts. Their testimonies will reshape the lenses you use to see what God is doing in our world today.

Jay Mātenga, DIS
Executive Director, World Evangelical Alliance Mission Commission

As an insider to this history, I am elated that what I know can now be public knowledge and more accessible. The record of God's move over the last two decades is nothing short of unbelievable. These writers chronicle a must-read book if you are committed to fulfilling the Great Commission.

Roy Moran
Chairman, Board of Directors
Global Platform Team Leader, New Generations

This book is compelling. Careful case studies illustrating that God is making millions of multiplying disciples globally can help skeptics and practitioners better understand that movements exist and are biblically sound. Thoughtful historical, biblical, and sociological analyses of disciple-making and the true nature of *ekklēsia* can help people be more effective. Challenging questions requiring careful consideration can help one avoid simplistic and formulaic approaches. The excellent final chapter responding to eight major objections to movements provides a great deal of detail and depth on how to both understand and answer these concerns.

S. Kent Parks, PhD
President and CEO, BEYOND

God is moving in unprecedented ways to start and grow over 2,000 movements to Christ around the world. The ongoing scholarly research of the Motus Dei network has been a gift to the global body of Christ. The initial book, *Motus Dei*, was focused on communicating primarily to academics and has been well received by many. However, the case studies and insights are too valuable to only share with academic communities. This book is a helpful adaptation of the original book that makes it more accessible to every reader (and will hopefully make it more feasible to translate into multiple languages). I strongly encourage you to read and pass on these stories of the amazing works of God in our generation.

STAN PARKS, PhD
Global Facilitation Team, 24:14
VP of Global Strategies, BEYOND

God on the Move is a primer on movement missiology for everyone—easily readable, refreshingly free of academic jargon, and presented in accessible, bite-sized portions. Yet it overflows with profound insight on the ancient-rediscovered ways God is bringing his kingdom to earth through movements. The stories will stir your spirit. The paradigms will offer you fresh lenses to view the world. After reading it, you may find yourself seeing the kingdom in entirely new ways and feeling, deep in your gut, a desire to step into these stories or live out your own God on the Move. I just love it!

EMANUEL PRINZ, DMin, PhD candidate
Affiliate Professor, Telos

A leading modernizing country experienced a convulsive revolution that resulted in the introduction of a government subject to a severe form of a compulsive, authoritarian, anti-Christian religion. Initial national euphoria was soon replaced by despair as the country slid into international isolation and social disintegration. Sixty-six percent of the dominant religion's worship centers emptied out. The national birth rate plunged to 30 percent below population sustainability. Initially Christianity flourished as an alternative to the repressive form of the national religion until the authorities ordered a crackdown to protect "national security." Traditional churches were compelled to close immediately. House churches numbered in many thousands were reduced to hundreds. Networking leaders urgently prayed and fasted. The Lord's response? "You were making converts not disciples. Converts run away during persecution but disciples are willing to die for me." Changes were made. Accelerated growth returned.

Wherever the focus shifts from "decision making" to "disciple making," unprecedented kingdom growth is occurring, especially in the most inhospitable environments. Missiologists calculate there are presently two thousand such movements underway. But a problem for busy practitioners in less fruitful or remote fields is accessing, adapting, and prioritizing their activities to benefit from this emerging information. Dave Coles, in *God on the Move: Making Disciples Among the Nations*, has done us all a great favor by summarizing and simplifying the more conceptually complex book *Motus Dei*. This distillation is pure gold for those lacking the luxuries of time, money, or access to digital libraries. Read this book. Be encouraged. Then dive into the swifter flowing current of disciple makers worldwide.

DR. STUART ROBINSON
Research Fellow, Melbourne School of Theology

This abridged version of *Motus Dei* is appropriate for those who want a broad introduction to the world of CPM/DMM without the deeper detail of the original version. Both versions are intended to take a more scholastic outsider's view. Most writing on the subject is either from the perspective of enthusiastic insiders or harsh critics who are reacting to what they have heard or perceived without much actual investigation. *God on the Move* is an attempt at a more neutral consideration of the phenomenon.

CURTIS SERGEANT
Disciple

God on the Move provides a clear description of the dynamics involved when Christ's church multiplies deep and wide in simple, reproducible, and sustainable ways around the world. Are you curious about movements? Start here.

BRUCE WILSON, DMin
Director of the Center for Church Multiplication,
Asbury Theological Seminary

God
ON THE
Move

Making Disciples Among the Nations

Dave Coles | Editor

Available at missionbooks.org

God on the Move: Making Disciples Among the Nations

© 2025 by Warrick Farah. All Rights Reserved.

No part of this book may be reproduced, stored in a retrieval system, or transmitted in any form or by any means—electronic, mechanical, photocopy, recording, or otherwise—without prior written permission from the publisher, except brief quotations used in connection with reviews. This manuscript may not be entered into AI, even for AI training. For permission, email permissions@wclbooks.com. For corrections, email editor@wclbooks.com.

William Carey Publishing (WCP) publishes resources to shape and advance the missiological conversation in the world. We publish a broad range of thought-provoking books and do not necessarily endorse all opinions set forth here or in works referenced within this book.

The URLs included in this book are provided for personal use only and are current as of the date of publication, but the publisher disclaims any obligation to update them after publication.

All Scripture quotations, unless otherwise indicated, are taken from the Holy Bible, New International Version®, NIV®. Copyright ©1973, 1978, 1984, 2011 by Biblica, Inc.™ Used by permission of Zondervan. All rights reserved worldwide. www.zondervan.com. The "NIV" and "New International Version" are trademarks registered in the United States Patent and Trademark Office by Biblica, Inc.™

Scripture quotations marked ESV are taken from the ESV® Bible (The Holy Bible, English Standard Version®), Copyright © 2001 by Crossway, a publishing ministry of Good News Publishers. Used by permission. All rights reserved.

Scripture quotations marked NKJV are taken from the New King James Version®. Copyright © 1982 by Thomas Nelson. Used by permission. All rights reserved.

Published by William Carey Publishing
10 W. Dry Creek Cir
Littleton, CO 80120 | www.missionbooks.org

William Carey Publishing is a ministry of Frontier Ventures
Pasadena, CA | www.frontierventures.org

Cover and Interior Designer: Mike Riester

ISBNs: 978-1-64508-667-3 (paperback)
   978-1-64508-669-7 (epub)

Printed Worldwide

29 28 27 26 25   1 2 3 4 5   OR 200

Library of Congress Control Number: 2025945001

CONTENTS

Foreword | Miriam Adeney — xi
Introduction | Dave Coles — xv

Part 1: What's Happening?

1. Fifteen Years of Disciple Making Movements | Samuel Kebreab — 3
2. Transferring Spiritual DNA in East Africa | Aila Tasse and L. Michael Corley — 17
3. Bhojpuri Case Study | Victor John with Dave Coles — 29
4. A Thai Multiplication Movement | Stephen Bailey — 43

Part 2: How Shall We Understand What's Happening

5. Discipleship Movements Today:
   A Primer from Multiple Perspectives | Warrick Farah — 53
6. "The Word of the Lord Spread Through the Whole Region":
   The Book of Acts and Church Planting Movements | Craig Ott — 73
7. God's Expanding Family:
   The Social Architecture of Ekklēsia Movements | Trevor Larsen — 83
8. But Is It Right?
   Answering Objections to CPM/DMM | Dave Coles — 95

FOREWORD

What a Holy Calling We Have Been Given

Miriam Adeney

Why should God care if I praise him? What is my voice among the billions of beings spinning through space? For whatever reason, my praise matters. Every person's does. Whether people are unfriendly, crude, and poor, or glamorous, gorgeous, and wealthy, every person on this earth is made in God's image, died for by Jesus, and called to live—filled with God's Spirit—for the kingdom of God in whatever niche they call home.

But how will those billions find out about this good news? How will they hear? When Paul preached in Antioch of Pisidia, "the word of the Lord spread through the whole region" (Acts 13:49). Later, when Paul ministered in Ephesus, "all the Jews and Greeks who lived in the province of Asia heard the word of the Lord," and learned that Jesus is the rightful Lord of the universe and Lord of our lives (Acts 19:10).

Could a message penetrate that widely today? That is the point of this book. Penetration is happening. Quietly and unobtrusively, millions of Muslims and Hindus, Buddhists and pagans, in some of the most unlikely places are coming to Christ as Lord. Equally impressive, those believers are sticking through persecution, growing in Christian knowledge and character, witnessing, and leading their own worship groups.

In other words, a tide is swelling. A surf is breaking. A wind is sweeping over the land. At the very beginning of time, the Spirit of God moved over the waters. At Pentecost, the Spirit of God moved over the disciples with tongues of fire. When there was great persecution, the Spirit of God moved Philip to walk south and bless the Ethiopian eunuch. In our time, this powerful but gentle force continues to flare over the earth. The Spirit is moving, people are being liberated, and God is being honored and adored.

Church Planting Movements (CPMs) are one key channel through which the Spirit flows. Today there are over two thousand CPMs, each defined as a group with at least one hundred congregations, planted by four successive generations of believers. Taken as a whole, these CPMs are populated by over one hundred million new followers of Jesus.

Each movement begins with prayer. Church planters listen to God and ask him for guidance and endurance and favor with their listeners. These witnesses are ordinary people, market vendors, truckers, and even former sex workers. Though they may lack training and credentials and financial resources, they do possess their own stories of new life and the grand meta-story revealed in Scripture.

Wherever they go, they look for a receptive host, a "person of peace" (Luke 10:5–7). In that person's home they meet regularly to tell a Bible story. These gatherings are interactive, asking, "What can we learn about God from this story? What can we learn about people?" Action-oriented, the sessions call for immediate application: "How can we apply what we've learned? Who can we share this story with this week?"

So from the first session, seekers become sharers, participants become witnesses.

Each person passes the stories around their own network, whose members then share them with their personal connections. In time new life swells, bursts forth, and multiplies, and as the good news streams down the lines of relationships, eventually there will be four "generations" of believers. Then five, then six, then seven, and on and on.

Each generation is discipled only by the preceding two or three, so hierarchy is kept minimal. New believers may not even know the names of the founding leaders. An accountability chart records the inquirers and committed followers. Such digital tracking encourages prompt and regular follow-up. Routine data collection like this fosters order, notes problems, and pushes priorities, because people value what they measure. For example, when Aila saw a list of all the unreached peoples in his native Kenya—twenty-six peoples—he determined to develop teams to bring the good news to every one of them. That data-prodded dream has come true.

"Discovery Bible Studies" can result in a "Disciple Making Movement." Quarterly meetings for regional leaders provide encouragement. To serve an unreached population, established churches in the area are invited to partner. Training is given, and collaboration guidelines are hammered out. While a counseling center in urban India or a noodle celebration in Thailand may build goodwill and open doors, the key remains the interactive communal Bible story shared in a receptive home, followed by active application.

But what about spiritually mature teachers? What about sound ecclesiology? What about heresy? Sincere Christians are right to raise such questions. These concerns are important and are tackled in chapter 8, titled "But Is It Right?"

There will come a day when we will go up to the city of God. The earth will be filled with the knowledge of the glory of the Lord like the waters cover the sea. The families of the earth will be blessed. The nations will shout for joy. East Africans will rise from their roast goat and spicy tomatoes and soft cheese with trilling ululations, men jumping exuberantly straight up and down. South Asians will rise from their naan and dal and hot masalas, Southeast Asians from their mangos and coconut cream. Cheers and whoops and bellows will resound the songs of souls who have been set free. Together as one royal priesthood, one holy nation, one people belonging to God, we will declare the praises of the One who has called us out of darkness into his marvelous light. No longer foreigners and aliens, but fellow citizens with God's people, we will be built together into a dwelling where God lives by his Spirit. Then we will gather from every nation and tribe and people and language around God's throne. Does God want our praise? He does. And at last, God will receive what he is due.

What a privilege to help make that happen. What a holy calling we have been given.

Miriam Adeney, PhD

INTRODUCTION

Dave Coles

A brother serving in West Africa once told me, "I wish there could exist a simplified version of the book *Motus Dei*, with excerpts especially relevant for field workers in my African context—and likely elsewhere. Many of the people I work with would probably never read the more academic sections, but some chapters could be incredibly useful to them."

That sanctified wish planted a seed in my heart that grew into a vision—a shorter, simpler version of *Motus Dei*, tailored for busy field workers and a broader audience. In the few years since the publication of *Motus Dei: The Movement of God to Disciple the Nations*, I've received numerous requests for portions of the book. I always encouraged them to buy the whole book. Now, nearly five years later, I've begun considering the realities of a broader global audience.

Motus Dei filled a gap in the literature on movements. After two decades of mostly anecdotal and popular-level descriptions of movements, *Motus Dei* provided a more robust and academically credible description of this phenomenon. It gave substantial insight into the big picture of movements, the missional theology of movements, and movement dynamics—along with significant case studies of movements happening in different locations.

With that solid foundation already laid and still available, I began to envision a shorter and easier-to-read book. Which parts would appeal to busy field missionaries interested in reading *Motus Dei* but lacking the time to dig so deeply into the issues? Which chapters might be eagerly devoured by nonnative speakers of English, passionate to know more about God's work in our day through movements?

I ran this brainstorm past my friend Warrick Farah and Vivian Doub at William Carey Publishers. Both responded favorably and gave a green light to pursue the book you now hold in your hand—a shorter, simpler version of *Motus Dei*. Other than this introduction, all its contents have been simplified (and occasionally updated) from selected chapters of *Motus Dei* and approved by the authors of those chapters. So, if readers of this book desire more depth or more complete substantiation of anything written here, they can likely find it in the complete version of *Motus Dei*. In some cases, this small book may serve as an appetizer for that full-course banquet.

I hope you will find this book readable, edifying, and inspiring. God is graciously doing great things among unreached peoples in our day—bringing salvation to millions and glorifying the name of Jesus. May your heart rejoice in reading this good news.

Dave Coles
davecoles.freemin.org

PART 1

What's Happening?

Fifteen Years of Disciple Making Movements

Samuel Kebreab

I first learned about Disciple Making Movements (DMMs) in 2006 during a difficult time. I was serving as our denomination's outreach coordinator. We had a church planting effort among the Yoma people (pseudonym), an unreached group in southern Ethiopia. We aimed to plant one hundred village churches in fifteen years. By 2006, in our seventh year, we had only planted seven churches. I felt discouraged, and our goal seemed impossible.

During the DMM training, I felt the ideas made a lot of sense. I heard personal stories of DMMs leading to thousands of churches and tens of thousands of followers of Jesus. I began to hope this could happen in our area if we followed the DMM principles.

Soon after, I started training and coaching our church planters using DMM principles. I also trained the few young Yoma men and women who had come to faith through our ministry. The work began to grow slowly but steadily. It grew especially through the young Yoma men and women who were part of the Yoma community. They started reaching out to their parents and other close relatives. By March 2009, these young Yoma were baptizing their close relatives and many others in the community. The number of village churches grew to fifty-four.

When I first wrote this chapter, the DMM among the Yoma people had continued for fourteen years. They had 5,672 followers of Jesus in 364 village churches, spanning seven generations of churches. In April 2020, the movement sent Yoma workers to a neighboring unreached group to engage them with DMM. We were thrilled to see a movement that started in one group spreading to another unreached group.

My story is just one of thousands of DMM stories, similar to stories in Acts. These inspire God's people to praise him as they learn about his kingdom growing. I worked for nine years as Africa Research Director for New Generations. This role allowed me to visit and closely watch movements in all five of our African regions. I also received reports on DMMs in other parts of the world.

This chapter will describe what our organization has observed over fifteen years. Since 2005, we have tried to start DMMs in fifty-six countries in Africa and Asia. These movements show Jesus at work. When people focus on Jesus's teachings, God often starts great movements.

We will focus in this chapter on the results in thirty-one African countries and one South Asian country. We use both numbers and stories to see what God is doing and to understand what we might be missing. The results of our research have greatly encouraged us and helped us assist other organizations.

Before sharing the data from these years, I want to describe the DMMs we have studied.

Features of Disciple Making Movements

New Generations created the term DMM to describe the spread of the gospel by making disciples who learn to follow God's word and quickly make other disciples who do the same. This leads to many churches being planted. A DMM is not just a strategy or program but a way of life and a ministry philosophy based on kingdom values modeled by Jesus in the Gospels.

DMMs Depend Heavily on Prayer, Often Followed by Miraculous Signs

Every DMM we have seen starts with intense prayer and fasting. Faith-filled prayers ask God to bring his kingdom into people's lives and entire villages and cities. This leads to changed lives, communities, towns, and cities. Jesus taught his disciples to pray for God's kingdom to come; this important prayer leads to kingdom results.

When Jesus's disciples went from village to village to share the kingdom message, he gave them the power to show signs of God's kingdom presence among the people. They shared the good news along with healing and deliverance. In DMM, we have seen the kingdom show itself through healing, deliverance, and other miraculous signs alongside sharing the gospel. We estimate that miraculous signs have happened in 50 to 70 percent of the times when movements have started.

DMMs Equip Ordinary People to Achieve the Impossible

DMMs are simple, easy to grow, and sustainable partly because they usually start with committed and obedient ordinary people. Some of our successful movement leaders have been housewives, poor widows, bicycle taxi drivers, masons, farmers, and former commercial sex workers. DMMs do not rely on highly skilled and educated outsiders to share the message. They rely on obedient insiders who may not have any special skills or education. They do not depend on resources from outside but can be sustained through what local people can afford and create (Matt 10:9–10). They do not lack workers because workers come from within the harvest field itself.

However, this does not mean there is no need for gifted and highly skilled outsiders to start, promote, or help a movement. In DMM, an outsider's main role is to equip ordinary people, who then do the work of starting, promoting, and helping the movement (Eph 4). The ministry model that depends on highly educated and paid clergy does not produce a simple, easy-to-grow, and sustainable movement.

DMMs Are Holistic: Combining Compassion and Healing with the Gospel of Kingdom Transformation

In Jesus's earthly ministry, we do not see a separation between sharing the kingdom message and showing compassion. The Gospel writers tell us that Jesus came to heal and preach. When he sent the Twelve to the villages to share the kingdom message, he gave them authority to heal and free people from evil spirits. DMMs follow the principle of entering communities with genuine love shown through compassionate ministry. This can include healing and deliverance or providing resources that help the whole community, like clean water, seeds, better health, better education, or skill development. Compassionate ministry is not an end in itself but is connected to our desire to see people come to know God. Compassion also helps us gain acceptance in the community and makes people willing to hear our message.

DMMs Trust God to Provide Resources Locally

Luke 10 and Matthew 10 describe two important resources God provides that help DMMs overcome cultural and financial barriers when entering a new area.

The first resource is God's preset person to bridge the gospel to their family, friends, community, or workplace. The Bible calls this person a "person of peace." These people are usually open to the gospel, welcoming, and willing to introduce their families to the gospel. The person of peace, whether a man or woman, breaks the cultural barrier. As a cultural insider, they do the inside work of promoting the gospel in their family, community, and tribe from day one.

The other provision is for field expenses. Jesus tells his disciples not to carry money when they go to the harvest field because everything they need will be provided for them there. This approach greatly reduces the money needed to make disciples and plant churches. The traditional way of making disciples and planting churches costs a lot of money that must come from outside. For example, David Barrett and Todd Johnson (2001, 520–29) estimate the total cost per baptism in the United States to be $1.55 million. In our case, all DMM expenses usually total much less than $100 for each person baptized, and most of these resources are provided locally.

DMMs Depend on Lost People Discovering God in the Bible and Choosing to Obey

We believe God is already working to prepare people's hearts (especially the person of peace). So, the harvest worker's job is to help lost people discover the truth from the Bible and obey it.

We call this method Discovery Bible Study (DBS). A DBS usually happens in a group and has four parts:

1. The group hears or reads a Bible passage or story in their own language.
2. Each person in the group retells the message in their own words.
3. Each person shares an "I will" statement, describing what they feel they should do in response to the passage and making a promise to obey it.
4. Each person lists the people they plan to share the passage with.

This way, from day one, we start making disciples who have a lifestyle of obeying God and making other disciples. People might start to obey God individually, in groups, or as a community. We call a group that meets regularly to hear God's word and intends to obey it a "discovery group." Besides studying the Bible together, a discovery group worships God together, prays for their needs and the needs of their community, and supports each other. They also check if members have followed their "I will" statements and shared what they learned in the previous lesson.

DMMs Involve Ordinary Disciples Making Disciples and Churches Planting Churches

One of the most important parts of DMM is the multiplication of disciples across generations, leading to the multiplication of churches. This creates a movement that will have a lasting result: reaching and changing communities, people groups, affinity groups, towns, and cities. This happens through sharing, showing, and experiencing the gospel. As the DMM progresses, most movements create their own natural structure that helps them organize and keep the movement growing. This differs from traditional methods in which the form and structure of a new church are decided by the mother church or denomination.

DMMs Require Courage and Sacrifice

Matthew 10:16–42 teaches us that suffering, persecution, and even martyrdom come with movements of kingdom advance. We have heard many stories of sacrifice in our fifteen-year DMM journey. However, this has not discouraged the Christians in these movements; instead, it has made them stronger. In most cases, persecution has not stopped movements. It has, instead, made people think more about the cost of discipleship and move on to new opportunities to bring change in the hardest places.

Data Collection Method and Data Verification Process

Data Collection Strategies and Methodologies

Our organization has a data and research team of eight people. Team members collect data and analyze the results of the DMM activities every quarter. We also collect DMM stories from each region every quarter.

Numerical data is checked for accuracy at the regional level by the regional data officer and then sent to the data team. Our quarterly data collection form has fourteen parts. The numerical information is entered into a CSV sheet and analyzed using Chartio, a cloud-based data analytics software. We compile the stories and activity reports and then analyze them to see the nature of the movement and the life changes happening among the people in the movement. As of the first quarter of 2020, we have DMM data for 655 people groups and seventy-seven urban centers and social segment groups from thirty African countries and one South Asian country.

Data Verification Process: Both Quantitative and Qualitative Data

We have a method to ensure the data we receive from the regions is reliable and accurate. Before it reaches the data team, data sent from the field by the church planter goes through at least three reviewers: the area coordinator, the country director, and the regional data officer. Each person checks the data for its reliability and accuracy. Questionable data is not submitted until it is verified.

Internal Audit and External Audit

Since 2012, we have been conducting ongoing internal audits by going to the field to do:

- Quantitative assessments—to determine the number of churches and followers.
- Qualitative assessments—to evaluate the DNA of the potential or actual movement.

In 2015, we invited an external audit to assess a country with remarkable outcomes. The International Mission Board's (SBC) Global Research Office performed that audit in 2016. The audited African country has many extraordinary DMMs happening. The IMB team chose nine people groups (seven of which were of Muslim background) to assess. The research group confirmed that strong DMMs are happening among these groups.

Now, we have started a comprehensive three-year process of internal audit called Internal Qualitative Assessment (IQA). We have designed the IQA to find out how much of the DNA of DMM has been passed from the first-generation disciple maker to the fifth-generation disciple or church.

Fifteen-Year Outcomes of 129 Movements (One Hundred or More Churches to at Least Four Generations) and Analysis of Some Key Elements

2005–2020 Third Quarter Summary Outcomes from Five African Regions and One South Asian Region

New Generations, working with more than 700 African and South Asian partner organizations, has seen God plant 79,862 churches among 605 people groups and 51 urban centers and social segments. Of the 79,862 churches planted, 29 percent have members from a Muslim background. The number of followers of Jesus is 1,858,531, with 32 percent from a Muslim background.

A total of 129 people groups, social segments, or urban centers have reached the DMM threshold. They have more than one hundred churches planted and four or more generations deep. The highest number of generations reached within one people group to date is thirty-four.

Table 1.1. New Generations' 15-Year DMM Totals

REGIONS WITH HARD DATA	NUMBER OF COUNTRIES ENGAGED WITH CHURCH PLANTING	TOTAL NUMBER OF PEOPLE GROUPS ENGAGED	NUMBER OF URBAN CENTERS AND SOCIAL SEGMENTS ENGAGED	TOTAL DMMs THAT REACHED MOVEMENT STAGE (>100 CHURCHES AND 4 GENERATIONS)	TOTAL NUMBER OF CHURCHES PLANTED	TOTAL NUMBER OF CHRIST FOLLOWERS
AFRICA	30	349	64	115	57,057	1,601,815
SOUTH ASIA	1	306	13	13	18,874	181,917
TOTALS OF HARD DATA REGIONS	31	655	77	128	75,931	1,783,732

Over the years, we have focused on engaging unreached or unengaged people groups who have no "Jesus option." As a result, the majority (61 percent) of the people groups we have engaged with DMM have been unreached people groups. We have intentionally made disciples in new places among people groups with no or few followers of Jesus.

Analysis of the 129 Movements That Have Reached the DMM Threshold

Most of the churches planted and the majority of the followers of Jesus are found in these 129 movements that have reached the DMM threshold. The number of churches in these DMMs is 60,767, which is 76 percent of the total number of planted churches. The number of followers in these DMMs is 1,602,195, which is 86 percent of the total followers. Therefore, the 129 DMM movements are a good representation of our organization's DMM work in Africa and South Asia. Let's look more closely at these movements. We have discovered the following:

1. Time Needed to Reach DMM Threshold

We found that, on average, it takes three and a half years (42 months) for a DMM engagement to reach the movement stage (one hundred churches and four generations). The time ranges from a minimum of 3 months to a maximum of 135 months (11 years and 3 months). However, out of the 129 movements, 70 percent reached the DMM threshold in less than four years. We did not find much difference between people groups with more than 2 percent evangelical population and those with less than 2 percent evangelical population.

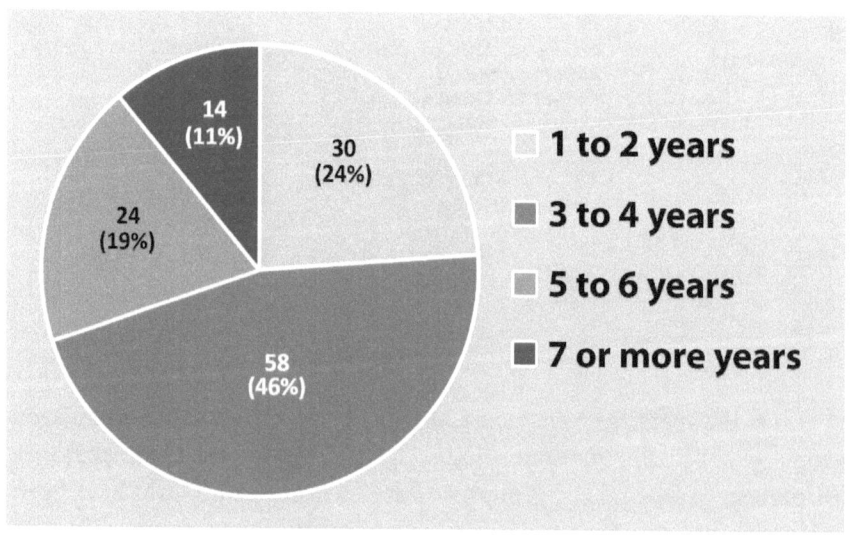

Figure 1.1. Number of people groups reaching DMM threshold

2. Numbers of Persons of Peace, DBS Groups, and Churches Planted

We analyzed the ratio of persons of peace to DBS groups to find out how many persons of peace are needed to start one DBS group. We found that 1.3 persons of peace needed to be found for one DBS group to start. In other words, for every four persons of peace found, three DBS groups formed.

Next, we looked at how many DBS groups were needed to plant one church. We found that 1.64 DBS groups were needed for one church. This means that roughly three DBS groups would lead to two churches.

Table 1.2. Number of DBS Groups in Regions

Region	Number of DBS Groups to Church
Anglophone West Africa Region	2.64 DBS groups for 1 church
Central Francophone Africa Region	0.99 DBS groups for 1 church
East Africa Region	1.9 DBS groups for 1 church
Horn of Africa Region	1.2 DBS groups for 1 church
West Francophone Africa Region	1.4 DBS groups for 1 church
South Asia Region	1.7 DBS groups for 1 church
Average	1.64 DBS groups for 1 church

3. Correlations Between Leaders Trained and Churches Planted, and Between Active Coaches/Trainers and Churches Planted

We analyzed in five sub-Saharan African (SSA) regions whether we could see a link between the number of leaders trained and the number of churches planted. We also looked at the link between the number of active coaches/trainers and the number of churches planted.

SSA: FOR EVERY TWO CHURCHES TO BE PLANTED ROUGHLY THREE DBSs NEED TO BE ESTABLISHED

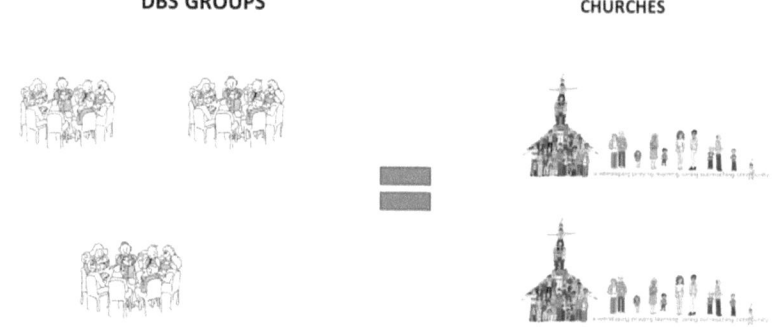

Figure 1.2. DBS per church plant

We found a strong positive correlation in both cases. The correlation coefficient between the number of leaders trained and the number of churches planted was 0.85629. The correlation coefficient between active coaches/trainers and the number of churches planted was 0.887808. This means that having more active trainers and coaches leads to planting more churches. In both cases, the relationship was statistically significant, with $p < 0.001$.

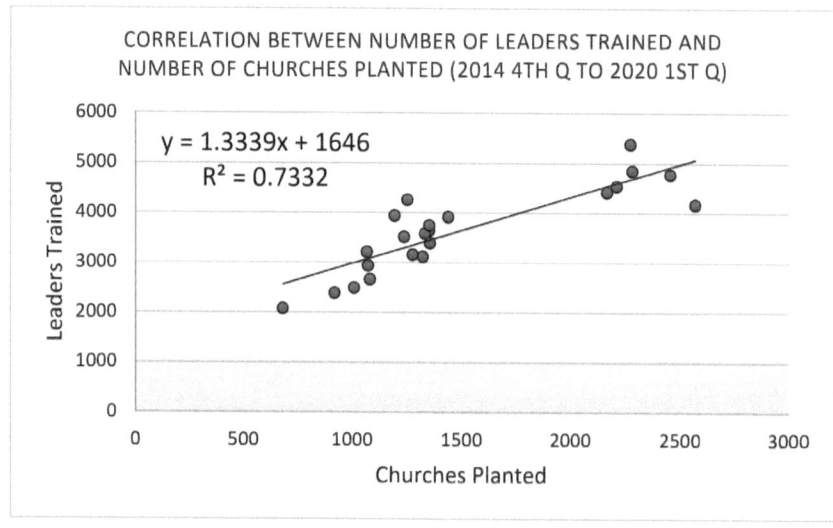

Figure 1.3. Correlation between leaders with church plants

Fifteen Years of Disciple Making Movements

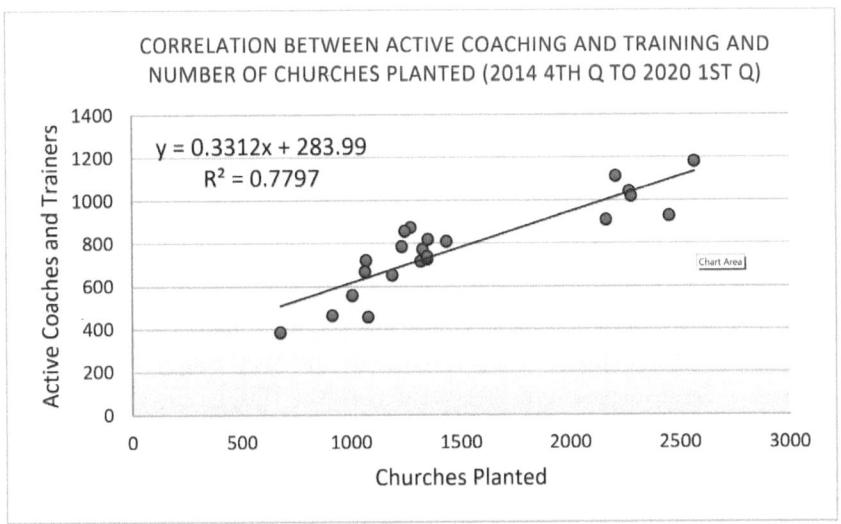

Figure 1.4.
Correlation between active coaching and training and number of churches planted

A Summary of Our Analysis

In our fifteen years on this DMM journey, we have learned that advancing God's kingdom can only happen by taking Jesus's teachings in the Gospels seriously and committing to obey him, no matter the cost. This is proven by the many people from different tribes, languages, peoples, and nations becoming followers of Jesus. We have seen Jesus's church formed in previously unreached places and people groups.

In the 129 movements, we analyzed how long it takes for a DMM engagement to reach the movement stage (one hundred churches and four generations). We found that most cases took less than four years. We also looked at the ratio of persons of peace to discovery groups and the ratio of discovery groups to churches. We found that for each discovery group, an average of 1.3 persons of peace is needed. For each church established, an average of 1.6 discovery groups is needed. In other words, finding roughly four persons of peace will produce three discovery groups, and three discovery groups will eventually become two churches. This "4 → 3 → 2" trend seems to be the rule in our case.

Figure 1.5. The 4–3–2 model

We also analyzed the link between the number of people being trained, coached, and mentored in DMM and the number of churches planted. We found that the more people are trained, coached, and mentored in DMM, the more churches are planted. As new leaders emerge from a new generation of a movement, they are trained and coached in DMM. This way, the DNA of the movement continues.

Conclusion

According to Rick Wood, "Christian history demonstrates one certain reality; the only way that peoples are ever reached is through movements" (2018, 4). The Gospels and Acts also confirm this truth, as does our experience over the past fifteen years.

In Matthew 28:18–20, Jesus commands his disciples to make disciples of all nations. The book of Acts shows how the disciples carried out this command. We read how something that started small, with the power of the Holy Spirit and the commitment of obedient disciples, became a movement that "turned the world upside down" (Acts 17:6 NKJV). God's kingdom impact was felt throughout the Roman Empire as leaders, disciples, and churches arose through the disciple-making process to continue making disciples everywhere.

While we don't claim that DMM is the ministry strategy in the New Testament, DMMs aim to work in the same spirit as Acts. We are amazed to see multitudes from many people groups becoming followers of Jesus, and we give credit to God for all the growth. We have learned firsthand that the harvest belongs to God, and the means and principles for gathering the harvest come from God. He is the one who sends harvest workers, even from the harvest field. Our part is to keep a teachable and obedient heart that responds to the Spirit's prompting as we work to glorify God's name among all people.

We know we are still beginners and have a lot to learn from God and his people. We also believe we have a duty to share God's mighty work of salvation among many lost people, which has happened before our eyes through the DMM process. We know the work is vast and the harvest is great. Therefore, we want more of the body of Christ to join us in the DMM journey. We long to see DMMs spread throughout the world until the earth is "filled with the knowledge of the Lord as the waters cover the sea" (Isa 11:9).

References

Barrett, David B., and Todd M. Johnson. 2001. *World Christian Trends, AD 30–AD 2200: Interpreting the Annual Christian Megacensus.* William Carey Library.

Wood, Rick. 2018. "Will We Hinder or Accelerate Movements? The Choice Is Ours." *Mission Frontiers* (March–April 2018).

2

Transferring Spiritual DNA in East Africa

Aila Tasse and L. Michael Corley

Aila traveled into Kenya's savanna, fasting and praying, "Tell me which way to go." He felt God's presence so strongly that he was afraid to open his eyes. In a vision, he saw a series of images like a slideshow. In the first image, he saw his hometown imam. Although this man had once been Aila's mentor, the imam had driven Aila away from his family after he became a Christian. When Aila saw his image, he thought, "I hate him." Still, God challenged him to pray for the imam and to bless him.

Next, Aila saw an image of his hated brothers and father, followed by slides of other groups. As painful memories of persecution rushed back, Aila released all his pent-up bitterness and felt a burden lifted off his chest.

In a second vision, he saw the Chalbi Desert—a place that had never had gardens, let alone cabbages. Yet in his vision, cabbages were not only sprouting but flourishing. Isaiah 43:18–19 flashed through his mind: "Forget the former things; do not dwell on the past. See, I am doing a new thing . . . I am making a way in the wilderness and streams in the wasteland." These visions of a harvest growing and thriving became Aila's burning bush. God called this former Muslim to reach not only his own people but also all neighboring tribes for Jesus.

For Aila, the image of flourishing cabbages symbolized a call to reach all people, regardless of their religion or culture. After reading Francis Omondi's *A Call to Share: The Unevangelised Peoples of Kenya*, he was shocked to learn that seventeen of Kenya's unreached people groups lived near him. He discovered, as John Piper writes, "The ultimate goal of God in all of history is to uphold and display his glory for the enjoyment of the redeemed from every tribe and tongue and people and nation" (1993, 228). God confirmed Aila's call to disciple all twenty-six of the unreached ethnic groups in his country.

This vision led to an interdenominational effort called Lifeway. The name comes from John 10:10 (ESV): "I came that they may have life and have it abundantly." When asked if he is a Christian, Aila replies, "I am a person of the Way. If you are on the Way, you will receive life." This is important because faithful Muslims pray many times a day, "Show us the straight way." For Aila, living an abundant life means focusing on mission rather than self-fulfillment. In its first ten years, Lifeway helped believers plant over 2,600 churches.

A Difficult Decision

The vision to see the unreached discover Jesus's abundant life moved Aila to give up everything. He was already a successful pastor with a church of one thousand and had already mobilized disciples to reach other tribes. So why risk losing something that was working? He realized that traditional methods for multiplying churches take too long, cost too much, and lead to little cultural change. Ultimately, he chose to obey Jesus.

Aila wondered, "How can my team and I see the spiritual DNA of a true follower of Jesus passed down from one generation to the next? Can this DNA spread to all these groups in my lifetime?" At first, he struggled to find an answer. He now believes we can see the Great Commission fulfilled in our lifetime if ordinary disciples are taught how to pass on that spiritual DNA.

For years, experts in discipleship and mission studies have supported the idea of multiplying disciples. However, many earlier methods were weakened by focusing on individual achievement, shallow spirituality, and a split between clergy and laypeople. When we talk about passing on the DNA of a movement, we mean more than just copying. We're saying to keep the true essence, not just produce a copy with mistakes. Sadly, too many churches create converts with spiritual defects instead of obedient followers of Jesus. Many "converts" never obey Jesus by making new disciples. They are like seedless grapes—the fruit is there, but it can't grow into a new vine. The key difference is the disciples' ability to reproduce because they remain connected to the source.

Lifeway leaders are passionate about mobilizing kingdom-minded disciples of Jesus—people of the Way. These disciples make more disciples, leading to churches that plant more churches. They see this as both normal and expected. In Jesus's parable, a seed falling on good soil has the potential to become another grape and even to grow into a whole vineyard. In the same way, each seed of a disciple has the potential to multiply into countless new generations when it stays connected to its source.

The Fruitful Way

In 2005, Lifeway partnered with New Generations (NG) to start, strengthen, and multiply movements. Together, they coined the phrase Disciple Making Movements (DMM). This label stresses the importance of passing on the qualities of an obedient follower of Jesus in a complete way. The collaboration among leaders acts as a trellis. It supports and encourages Lifeway and other movement leaders to maximize their fruitfulness by passing on Jesus's way.

Lifeway faced many challenges in multiplying movements. These included differences in cultures and religions, hard-to-reach locations, and the pull of the traditional Western ministry model. Aila led his team to overcome these barriers by apprenticing himself to Jesus as a lifelong learner of the Way. By mid-2020, his partners had mobilized others to engage 113 people groups. These included urban and special-interest groups in ten East African countries. Thirty-six of these engagements had reached movement status. This designation means they had planted at least one hundred churches with at least four generations of multiplication. Seven more engagements were at the tipping point, eleven midway to movement, and forty-five still in the early stage.

In just fifteen years, seventeen of the thirty-six DMMs in East Africa were in Kenya alone. As of 2020, Lifeway teams had planted 12,555 churches made up of 271,695 disciples. Five years later, by the first quarter of 2025, Lifeway teams had planted 25,859 churches with over 420,000 disciples in seventy-three DMMs in the East Africa and Southern Africa regions. In many of NG's regions, such as these, we see unengaged, unreached people groups being reached for the first time.

Lifeway uses an engagement-status grid to help leaders set goals for prayer, training, and resources. This grid helps each engagement become a movement. It is a key tool in their three-dimensional evaluation method. It pictures all three markers in one location: qualitative, quantitative, and sustainability.

A Way for All People Groups

Scholars have noted that most movements occur in societies isolated from outsiders, filled with uncertainty, where people worship in their own heart language. Yet Aila's experience shows that even with different social conditions, thirty-six people groups in East Africa have reached movement status. New followers come from many other cultures, religious backgrounds, and economic situations; not all have the Bible in their language. The key is that these groups have found effective lifestyles that overcome barriers. Disciples are being replicated, and churches are forming with similar spiritual DNA in all these previously unreached groups. They are not forming one after the other, but all at once, and not just because of expert cultural adaptation.

Lifeway avoided conflicts over cultural adaptation by not focusing too much on it. One of Aila's mentors, David Watson, advises disciple-makers to "deculturalize, not contextualize, the gospel" (Watson and Watson 2014, 9). This approach means using only Scripture for teaching and letting local people answer questions about it rather than simply hearing our answers. Aila's team points to the authority of Scripture, which allows each new group to listen directly to God's word. As a result, local believers are encouraged to ask, "What must we change in our lives and culture to obey all the commands of Christ?" This approach has helped activate the priesthood of all believers.

Jerry Trousdale also suggested a strategy where local disciples sharing the same geography, culture, or language focus on reaching hard-to-reach groups. As L. D. Waterman wrote, "Outsiders can suggest relevant passages for study and provide outside mentoring for the group facilitator. But the onus of application is on the cultural insiders" (2017). Existing leaders then work to raise up new leaders within their own group to reach movement status.

Another barrier to movements is found in societies deeply influenced by Christianity. Some leaders were discouraged from training denominations because they struggled to understand and adopt DMM and break away from tradition. Despite this, some leaders, like Aila, did train them. Over five hundred partner organizations and denominations now work with NG in sub-Saharan Africa. Many of the more than twelve thousand churches were started in Kenya, one of Africa's most Christian countries. Lifeway has engaged all twenty-six of Kenya's unreached groups and even some of its least reached groups. Aila's team is committed to mentoring, training, and loving these groups so they can hear directly from God about transforming their communities.

Transferring the Spiritual DNA of Movements

The biggest challenge has been overcoming centuries of an individual-focused, information-heavy Western approach to discipleship. This approach limits true multiplication. After twenty-five years, many now see movement thinking not as a passing fad but as an ancient, biblical way to make disciples. DMM supporters believe we should return to the way Jesus worked, not just copy what the apostles did as viewed through a Western lens. As Trousdale put it, "What Jesus did . . . his disciples still do" (Trousdale and Sunshine 2018, 161). We believe we should follow Jesus's ministry model. The New Testament shows a rapid expansion into many areas at once. The world was "turned upside down" as his disciples passed on the kingdom's DNA (Acts 17:6). This growth was messy and imperfect, yet it was nurtured to maturity through personal coaching and teaching from the Epistles.

Evaluation of Movements

A good shepherd counts his flock and checks for problems. Our leaders use both quality measures and statistical indicators to evaluate the "spiritual DNA" of movements. We look at three parts: qualitative, quantitative, and sustainability indicators.

Qualitative factors help us check if the replication is healthy. We look at the number of generations from the original group to see if the DNA is being passed on faithfully. Our goal is four generations, which indicates the DNA is healthy and replicating.

In 2 Timothy 2:2, Paul shared a vision of teaching and spreading the message across at least four generations. He encouraged Timothy to train trustworthy leaders who could also share the good news and teach others. Instead of Timothy only focusing on helping one person at a time, he and his team were encouraged to train groups of leaders who could go on to guide and teach even more people. In Western cultures, this often means focusing on individuals. However, movements focused on growth aim to reach entire families, tribes, and communities—and sometimes individuals.

This focus leads to measuring how well a group can keep growing and teaching others without outside help. A key goal is to see seven generations of teaching and growth. Once this happens, teams like Lifeway step back a little, providing less financial help and spending less time directly involved. By this point, the group has grown enough to continue without outside leaders. The focus shifts from hands-on help to offering advice and mentoring from a distance.

Quantitative factors help us see impact, like the number of new churches started. We consider a movement to have at least one hundred new churches with at least four generations of replication. These levels imply the gospel has gone viral. These numbers help leaders know when to coach, train, and provide resources. We don't just count event attendance or donations. We focus on how many people live on mission by praying, serving, and making disciples. Measuring these things helps determine if a chain reaction is happening. Are disciples making disciples as an active priesthood of believers? Is this resulting in a cascade of churches planting churches? If so, this is a movement. As of 2020, 128 of NG's 651 global engagements had reached movement status. By God's grace, as of the first quarter of 2025, 330 out of 1,104 engagements have reached movement status.

Other factors also contribute to deciding when to step back, like building strong inside leaders, worshiping in the local language, and funding training and community projects coming from within the group. The 24:14 Coalition uses "streams" to check how healthy a movement is. A stream is like a chain of churches, unique in connection or location, that needs its own plan and attention to grow successfully.

We use a three-dimensional (3D) approach to evaluation:

1. Deep—Depth of relationships
2. Wide—Magnitude of reach
3. Long—Sustainability factors

3D evaluation helps leaders understand what must always be present in disciples to ensure accurate replication. The exact numbers are not the most crucial part. What matters most are skilled workers who listen to what the Lord says about leading his flock. We also include these evaluation ideas in our training. When ordinary disciples are trained, coached, and evaluated, they help leaders adjust the movement as needed.

Passing on the spiritual DNA creates a new generation of believers with the same quality. Just as a vineyard with good DNA still needs careful pruning to produce fruit that can grow new vines, the spiritual DNA must be nurtured. We all know what happens in the "Telephone Game" when a message gets messed up while being passed along. The same problem can occur if a middle person stops disciples from hearing directly from God and his word. The challenge is to ensure that what is passed on stays true to the biblical model.

Research Methodology

Our local leaders measure the size, depth, and sustainability of movements. We decided to conduct an Internal Qualitative Assessment (IQA) to study and improve the quality of this spiritual copying. Local people lead the IQA, which is relational and helps us decide about leading the flock.

We chose a grounded theory approach to discovering the key features of spiritual DNA in movements. This approach focuses on what is being studied rather than the methods, and it includes the interviewer's thoughts and notes. Researchers came in with an open mind to learn from ordinary people.

They asked these three main questions:

- What qualities of spiritual DNA mark a DMM in individuals, churches, leaders, and movements?
- How is spiritual DNA transferred effectively from one generation to the next?
- What external and internal factors help or hinder the passing of this DNA in a DMM?

Out of seventeen Kenyan movements, we did a pilot IQA in two of them.

- **Group A** is in the northwest along the Uganda-Ethiopia border. They are Nilotic pastoralists, known as fierce warriors, with a population of over one million. Most follow ethnic religions, though 5 percent are mainline Christians. Lifeway's work with Group A started in late 2010, and by early 2020, 404 churches had been planted through seven generations, with 24,038 followers.

- **Group B** is a 97 percent Muslim group in northern Kenya. They are connected to a larger group in southern Ethiopia, consisting of over one hundred thousand people. Lifeway began working with Group B in the third quarter of 2010, and by early 2020, 503 churches had been planted through eight generations, with 15,090 followers.

Table 2.1. Engagement Status

LEGEND	LEVEL I	LEVEL II	LEVEL III	LEVEL IV
MOVEMENT STAGE		100+ churches and 4 generations	100+ churches and 5-6 Generations	100+ churches and 7+ generations
TIPPING POINT STAGE	67-99 churches and 1-2 generations	67-100+ churches and 3-4 generations	67-99 churches and 5-6 generations	67-99 churches and 7+ generations
MIDWAY TO MOVEMENT STAGE	34-66 churches and 1-2 generations	34-66 churches and 3-4 generations	34-66 churches and 5-6 generations	34-66 churches and 7+ generations
PIONEERING STAGE	1-33 churches and 1-2 generations	1-33 churches and 3-4 generations	1-33 churches and 5-6 generations	1-33 churches and 7+ generations

Five churches were evaluated in each movement. We used six individual interviews, a focus group of six to eight people per church, and participant observation at each church gathering. Each pilot included about seventy interviews and ten observations.

In the future, our Global Analytics Team will code all interviews from East African movements and other regions to complete an evaluation of six movements. This coding will help us build our grounded theory about how spiritual DNA is passed along in movements.

While our analysis is ongoing, we share some initial findings from the first two movements. These early findings show unique ways that new disciples see Jesus, themselves, and the mission he gave us. The results show a shared, community-based approach to their spiritual journey on "The Way."

Initial Observations from the IQA

The Way Is a Person

While Christians around the world say Jesus is "the life," these Kenyan churches often say Jesus is "the Way." Many interviewees repeated, "Jesus is the way and the source of eternal life," quoting John 14:6: "I am the way, the truth, and the life." People from many different backgrounds connect with Jesus in this way. This Way includes men, women, children, Muslims, animists, those who can read, and those who cannot. Evaluating the DNA of disciples in later generations, we found that talking about God is the most essential part of their daily lives. They talk about God with great confidence. One said, "God is great. He is love, Savior, and I followed him." Believers shared it was God's love that made them "believe and get baptized." One Muslim-background believer explained, "I learn good things from him: the example, love, and mercy of Jesus." This shows that the gospel is about declaring who God is, based on what he did in Jesus Christ.

The Way Is a Lifestyle

Following Jesus on the Way is not just about choosing certain beliefs; it is a lifestyle of discovery and making disciples. For both movements, "Following Jesus means doing good deeds." Their selfless love and actions are crucial in passing on the spiritual DNA. As Kierkegaard said, "Christ did not appoint professors, but followers. If Christianity is not lived out, it is not truly explained" (quoted in Rohde 1988, 117). These churches do not rely on official evangelism or charity programs but live out a life of loving God and people. They express inspiration from following Jesus's ways, which they say fills their lives with joy. While many call this "evangelism," those in DMM live out their faith with compassion and prayer for healing, leading others to be drawn to God. As they intercede for a breakthrough, God leads them to a person of peace who is being drawn to God. This path bears fruit as disciples surrender everything to follow Jesus and introduce others to him.

The Way Is a Communal Journey

An unexpected finding was that following Jesus as "the Way" is a group journey of learning and sharing. Both movements emphasized a shared experience of loving God through a personal relationship with Jesus, not just learning about him. They stay connected with the Way and invite others to join. A strong part of DMM is asking, "Would you like to gather with your family and friends to study God's word?" They start DBS in their own social circles. One interviewee said, "We come together because of DBS to learn and fellowship from house to house." As people explore their faith, their idea of the Way often overlaps with being a disciple—an individual who learns from the master and then helps others. This view contrasts with many Western approaches where discipleship is seen as private. These Kenyans view the Spirit's power as given primarily for reaching the lost together.

The Way Brings Transformation and Crosses Barriers

Another discovery is that the gospel's power to change lives overcomes barriers. Jesus said our love for others is our true mark (John 13:35). These followers show unconditional love—not just to win converts but to truly change lives. One woman even intentionally moved to a new village and lowered her hairdressing prices to serve the poor. Actions like these help people to "see the gospel." Ordinary disciples show Jesus's way through their love. This happens especially when they break negative patterns, like domestic abuse or tribal conflicts. Changes like these make people curious to know *why*.

Many churches also reported miracles, such as people being set free from evil spirits or healed from blindness and deafness. All the churches in pilot number 1 shared a miracle, even though the questions did not mention miracles. These miracles, which result from caring and prayer, confirm that the gospel is not just human but from God.

However, the greatest miracle is the empowerment of ordinary disciples. Rejecting the tradition that only clergy can teach, all disciples are challenged to launch a DBS. Working within social networks enables the gospel to transfer readily. This unleashing of God's people brings the great miracle of a life-giving Way in the desert. The result is disciples from all walks of life embracing Jesus.

The Way Involves Groups Discovering and Obeying Together

Our research also found that group discovery and group obedience are significant. The church shows God's kingdom when believers gather. When groups study God's word and live out the teachings of King Jesus, their communities are transformed much more than when people work alone. In these movements, "learning" means discovering truth by directly interacting with Scripture. Jesus asked many questions and taught using parables, which made people think deeply. In these groups, leaders answer questions with more questions. This strategy encourages everyone to retell Scripture in their own words. Focusing on the text and shared discovery leads to a powerful disciple-making revolution.

God wants all people to worship, love, and obey him. We work with him by starting DMMs. The true game-changers are not just those who believe in Jesus but those who obey him. The Great Commission will be accomplished by ordinary disciples trained and empowered to listen to God and make disciples who plant churches. These believers leave their meetings ready to help others obey Jesus and transform their communities.

> DMM leaders worldwide train followers that God is the one who teaches everyone (John 6:43–45). If the ultimate authority is the word and not the opinion of a pastor or facilitator, then believers can hold one another accountable to God's way. During the Reformation, we got the priesthood of the believer half right. . . . The half we got right is that we do not need a priest to talk to God. The half we are still working on is that we also do not need a priest for God to speak to us. (Forlines 2017)

When disciples hear from God and live it out, they set an example for others to follow. As the saying goes, "Most truth is caught, not taught." When believers show unity and love, others learn from them and are transformed. Even their fellowship and unity have a missional focus. They often ask the question, "How can we obey this together?" People respond when a community of people actively loves a family far from God. These group dynamics increase ownership, long-term memory, and impact among those they serve. People are affected deeply when disciples imitate Jesus's life and follow him together.

Conclusion

In December 2019, Aila and his team went into the mountains to hold a DMM training with his country's last unreached people group. While they were there, violence spread from a neighboring country. One of Aila's Lifeway friends and co-trainers was killed in the crossfire.

Achieving the vision of cabbages growing in the desert has come at a high cost. But Jesus's love drives disciples to find his joy while walking this narrow path of reconciliation—even if it passes through dark valleys. It is the Way of Jesus, from life to life.

By training shepherds to evaluate the movement, leaders create a pattern that shows the movement's true nature while allowing for unique local expressions. These leaders then protect that pattern and pass it on to the next generation. If we fail to keep and inspire the proper transfer of spiritual DNA, the gospel may become diluted, or the mission may decline. Balancing these factors is key to long-lasting fruitfulness. Harry Brown, president of NG, often says, "Our legacy is not what we can do ourselves, but what future generations of disciples will believe and do when we are long gone."

References

Forlines, James. 2017. "When Disciple Making Movements Are Misunderstood." Mission Frontiers (November–December). www.missionfrontiers.org/issue/article/when-disciple-making-movements-are-misunderstood.

Piper, John. 1993. *Let the Nations Be Glad! The Supremacy of God in Missions.* Baker Book House.

Rohde, Peter P., ed. 1960, 1988. *The Diary of Soren Kierkegaard.* Kensington Publishing.

Trousdale, Jerry, and Glenn Sunshine. 2018. *The Kingdom Unleashed: How Jesus' 1st-Century Kingdom Values Are Transforming Thousands of Cultures and Awakening His Church.* DMM Library.

Waterman, L. D. 2017. "Different Pools, Different Fish: The Mistake of 'One Size Fits All' Solutions to the Challenge of Effective Outreach Among Muslims." Fuller Seminary. Global Reflections. https://sparks.fuller.edu/global-reflections/2017/01/18/different-pools-different-fish-the-mistake-of-one-size-fits-all-solutions-to-the-challenge-of-effective-outreach-among-muslims/.

Watson, David, and Paul Watson. 2014. *Contagious Disciple Making: Leading Others on a Journey of Discovery.* Thomas Nelson.

3

Bhojpuri Case Study

Victor John with Dave Coles

A full description of the Bhojpuri Church Planting Movement (CPM) is available in the book *Bhojpuri Breakthrough: A Movement that Keeps on Moving* (John and Coles 2019). Some quotes from the book have been simplified with permission from the publisher.

In this chapter, we will focus on just two aspects of the movement:

1. What was unique about the Bhojpuri context, and how did the movement handle it?
2. What leadership features of the movement are countercultural?

What Was Unique About the Bhojpuri Context, and How Did the Movement Handle It?

Several things make the Bhojpuri movement different from many other CPMs listed by the 24:14 Coalition. Some of these elements are also found in other movements, but many are not common in most current movements. This combination makes the Bhojpuri movement unique.

The Movement Started in the 1990s, Before the Term CPM Became Defined or Described

Some important ideas for starting the Bhojpuri movement came from a training session for strategy coordinators in 1994. "The idea behind the Bhojpuri vision was to get rid of the old-fashioned way of evangelism and church planting that focused too much on specific areas. We didn't start with a fixed plan for how the ministry would grow; everything has been changing over the years" (11–12).

The Movement Grew in an Area Previously Called the "Graveyard of Missions"

"In the past, this region was very hostile to the gospel, which was seen as foreign. It was known as 'the graveyard of missions.' When the foreignness was removed, people started accepting the good news" (3).

> I had heard about the missionaries who had worked in the Bhojpuri area before—their hard work, failures, and successes. I wondered, "If all this work only produces small results, what's the solution? What is stopping the missionaries from seeing big success?" Even though the missionaries had significant resources, training, and strong partnerships, they weren't reaching their goals. This made me think about my own efforts: "Am I asking the right questions? Or am I actually offending the non-Christians around me?" (6)

From this struggle came a new way to share the gospel among the Bhojpuri people.

The Movement Started and Has Continued in an Area Where Some Legacy Churches Already Existed[1]

As more movements began in the decades since the 1990s, we saw that movements often grow best in places where Christianity was not well known before.

In places with many legacy churches, new movements have trouble sustaining movement dynamics and multiplying to four or more generations. New believers might feel (or be told by members of existing churches) that "to be a real Christian, you should worship every Sunday in a church building. You should be part of a large group led by a pastor from a recognized denomination." What happens when the standard for Christian life becomes just going to church once a week instead of actively following Jesus every day? Spiritual excitement fades, and rapid growth slows down to just a few new members. Spiritual breakthrough fades into just maintaining what already exists.

---

1 "Legacy churches" have already existed for a significant length of time. They are usually characterized by ownership of a designated church building, leadership by an ordained person, a significant element of biological and/or transfer growth in their membership, and patterns of worship and ministry following norms common in long-established Western churches.

In the Bhojpuri area, legacy churches were mostly made up of and led by people from the lower parts of society. In India's caste-based society, this meant lower-caste people. Because of this, many church leaders had no background, support, or examples of good leadership. Many missionaries only reached people who had little influence in their communities—not the decision-makers. These people became good Christians, but they didn't have leadership qualities. Nothing in their lives or caste backgrounds gave them the confidence to lead.

> On the positive side, missionaries brought the good news and hope to the lowest people in society, and they tried to spread the good news widely. They created a Christian identity, but it still depended on foreigners and lacked local leadership. Indian Christians remained very dependent on foreign workers and resources. They believed that only Western missionaries could share the gospel or lead a church. (4–5)

In Northern India, the few Christians were especially weak and dependent. They were a tiny minority in a vast sea of Hindus and Muslims. The mindset was "us vs. them." "Us" meant a small minority lacking resources and strong leadership. So, they focused on surviving as Christians rather than sharing their faith with others. People were suspicious of non-Christians who came to the churches. Their deep suspicion stopped them from wanting to reach out to others.

> The church in India was also very Western in language, culture, and worship style. They didn't connect with most of the people around them. Instead of using the local Hindi word for God, they used the English word. This kind of Christianity was the only Christian message available up through the early 1990s. It didn't offer real hope for reaching the Bhojpuri or other groups in Northern India. (5–6)

All these factors made it hard for legacy churches to effectively reach most people. However, in many cases, we have been able to help and encourage pastors of these churches. At the start of our vision-casting process, we invited all nearby pastors and church leaders to the first Bhojpuri Consultation, held in Varanasi in 1994. Since then,

> Over the past twenty plus years, countless . . . pastors have experienced a . . . shift: from frustration to fruitfulness. Many formerly frustrated and depressed leaders now have abundant

ministries reaching the lost. The movement includes some pastors previously confined to one location with just a few believers in a small church. Through a simple change of approach and some mentoring, they have grown amazingly and now minister in two or three different districts, mentoring many other leaders. (157)

"We mentor not only field workers but also traditional pastors. The Lord has allowed us to influence them toward simpler, more repeatable church patterns" (172). We have found that our holistic approach has greatly helped pastors who had previously faced persecution and protests when using a direct evangelistic approach.

The Movement Has Mainly Reached Hindus, Yet It Hasn't Been Limited to One Caste or Another

"In India's society as a whole, caste still plays an important role. It causes social tensions and supports Hindu fundamentalism" (22). Yet, "among the Bhojpuri, God is now working among every caste, even with lower-caste people reaching upper-caste people. Believers from different castes might not hang out much with each other, but they have worship meetings together and pray together" (25).

The Bhojpuri movement has made a big difference in this caste-driven society. The Bhojpuri area has 20 percent high-caste people and 80 percent low-caste or outcast Dalits and *Adivasi*. The good news has entered the low-caste 80 percent of the population more quickly, so the church reflects that social reality. This means we have had to address real issues related to caste (23).

> We focus on reaching people based on their language, location, and economic status, rather than caste. This helps the good news to take root throughout the region and spread. Caste divides groups, but language brings people together, so we have chosen not to focus on caste. (24)

The Movement Uses a Flexible Access Structure Called Community Learning Centers (CLCs)

These build trust for workers entering new areas. God has called us to start planting fellowships in whole communities. CLCs have opened many doors for achieving this goal. A CLC allows leaders to focus on reaching lost people and effectively connect with them. Through the CLC, we show

Christ's love to people who might otherwise never hear the good news or see it lived out in their context.

Our first CLCs opened in 2008, and these changed how we develop leaders. We train local leaders to

1. act as agents of change,
2. use the CLC programs to help all people (Gal 6:10), and
3. find the "person of peace" (Luke 10:5; Matt 10:11) in their local communities.

CLC leaders meet community needs and solve local problems. This builds strong relationships in the community, always aiming to advance God's kingdom.

> CLCs use a holistic approach to serving. Each CLC aims to provide access to the community, find the person of peace, and offer resources. It then implements locally relevant services and meets people's needs where they live. When needs are met, the good news of the Kingdom finds fertile ground, and CLC leaders can start making disciples and multiplying. Using the CLC approach, the good news has been planted in places that were previously barren. (33)

For example, during the COVID-19 pandemic in 2020, many CLC leaders were able to use the goodwill they had gained through their CLC to help people in need. Even during lockdown, they worked with police and government officials to distribute food, masks, and hygiene kits. Many held awareness programs and increased awareness in creative ways. In some cases, this opened doors to new contacts. Some also helped needy people open bank accounts to receive benefits from the government's relief program. In a tough sociopolitical time, all these activities brought significant goodwill within communities and appreciation of the ministry by Jesus's followers.

The Movement Has Seen Many Miraculous Healings, Including Some People Being Raised from the Dead

Many movements have experienced miraculous healings and deliverances, but not many have seen people raised from the dead. Yet miraculous signs have never been the main focus of the movement. "Signs and wonders also play a significant role in this movement, but they are just part of God's great work" (xvi). "In our context, signs and wonders always happen wherever the gospel is preached. Miracles happen quite often in the movement, but we don't focus on them. We focus on obeying God and doing what he commands to show his glory on earth" (198).

The movement uses Discovery Bible Studies (DBS) a lot for the growth and spiritual development of believers. However, DBS is not used with unbelievers. This is unique because in other movements, DBS is usually used with unbelievers and continues after they come to faith (Coles and Parks 2019, 315). In the Bhojpuri movement, finding a person of peace in each location is important, but that person does not usually start a DBS with unbelievers. They create relationships with their family, friends, and community, through which the gospel is shared and shown.

The Movement Began in Rural Areas and Has Also Successfully Spread to Urban Areas

Most CPMs today have spread mainly in rural areas. India has a huge number of people who haven't heard the gospel in both rural and urban areas. "As God blessed the movement among the Bhojpuri and we shared our work with others, some people challenged us: 'All your ideas work in the village but they won't work in the city'" (John and Coles 2019, 103–4).

Urban work is different from rural work in many ways. Rural work is community based, with more similar groups, so it's easier in one way. Urban work tends to be broken up and disconnected. Most people aren't local; they have moved from villages or other states, so the community has many layers to consider.

In rural areas, you often meet the same people in the same places, and change happens slowly. Even when people move away, their families stay. Cities are more temporary. In urban work, when someone moves, they disappear; the whole family relocates. We had to overcome this big challenge (105).

The movement's start in urban ministry "began with prayer and research, which worked together. Prayer guides the research and gives wisdom to understand and use the research results. Each group and area is unique. Research shows important information about people's main concerns and possible ways to reach them" (106).

Our research showed that the fast-paced lifestyle and rapid growth of the city had created many serious social problems. These include depression, suicides, rapes, divorces, juvenile crimes, murders, broken families, and immoral relationships. . . . Our research found many young people moving to Delhi for study and other reasons. Many faced loneliness, isolation, stress, identity crises, and culture shock (108).

We wanted to respond to the needs we had found through prayer and research. So, "we opened a counseling center at a nearby mall, where over seventeen hundred young people have visited each year since it opened" (109).

This provides access to the youth and allows us to find persons of peace (Luke 10). This person of peace strategy had already worked well among the Bhojpuri. People in urban areas often have little free time. So, we have found small gatherings (nontraditional worshiping communities) very effective because they are more flexible (109).

More recently, we have spread our urban ministry, increasing the number of young people being reached. We now have over twenty-five different centers where leaders are working in different urban areas.

The urban work became very successful for the following reasons:

1. We had a proven model working among the Bhojpuri. We used CPM principles and access ministry to bless people and find a person of peace. That person then became the key to reaching their network of relationships.

2. God helped us do research and pray, guiding us to learn effective ways to reach people. Urban approaches needed to be different from rural ones.

3. We didn't wait for people to come to us. We actively reached out to people. Through the counseling work, we went to schools and colleges. We held awareness programs on important topics like child abuse, sexual abuse, and career options. These programs were well-received by young people. (111–12)

One more thing worked well in the urban context:

Both group and individual approaches have been very successful in Delhi. In both cases, finding a person of peace is key. If I find one person who is open, I want to help them see their workplace or school as a place to reach others. So that person of peace starts reaching out to their contacts. These urban "communities" are completely different from rural communities, but the good news is spreading among them. (113)

India Has a Unique Social Problem with Children Being Abandoned (or Running Away)

"Thousands of abandoned children live at railway stations across India. They usually sleep only 2–3 hours a day because they fear robbery, rape, and beatings" (xii). As we help them, we aim to reunite them with their families whenever we can. "From the very beginning, our main principle has been: 'When we help children, whether orphaned, semi-orphaned, or street children, we don't want to create a warehouse of children'" (88). "In our work with railway children, we focus mainly on restoring them to their families. We talk with them to find out where they came from, who they are, and how they ended up there. Then we work with the government and the police to bring them back to their families" (89).

India Has Huge and Widespread Social Diversity

"When you travel even five to ten miles in India, you often find differences in dialect and culture" (165). To respond to this diversity, our ministry uses repeatable training that can easily be customized.

Because of this diversity, it's better for leaders to use their own examples instead of just repeating what we say. Our teaching doesn't force information on them; it involves discussion and discovery together. We use a group learning process, so we, as trainers, also learn. Everyone shares their experiences and what they have learned, and new ideas come as the Lord directs (165).

We teach a little, then they do it and learn from their experience as well as from our teaching. This helps them work effectively. When they learn from us, that starts the process. When they start using what they learned, they learn even more things because God is teaching them. What they learn from God, they learn much better. When they teach others, they share what we taught plus what God taught them (165).

This approach allows for repeatable yet customized training throughout the movement.

Contextually Using Bhojpuri Language and Culture Has Played a Key Role in the Movement's Fruitfulness

"It's not that attempts to reach the Bhojpuri suddenly started in the 1990s. But those doing the outreach hadn't used the Bhojpuri language in their approach. . . . When we talk now about the Bhojpuri language, it's a key part of our strategy—a very different way of thinking" (6). Using local music and life rituals has also strengthened believers' gatherings and opened doors to share the gospel. "The Bhojpuri songbook has written guidelines for events like marriage, childbirth, death, Holy Communion, child dedication, a child's birthday, an anniversary, baptism, and so on" (185). Here is one specific example of effective outreach:

> Some groups have a ceremony a certain number of days after a person's death. This ceremony is done in a Christian way with prayer, not with the old rituals. We don't necessarily stop the traditional gatherings, but instead of mourning, we celebrate. People invite all their relatives to the ceremony and share the good news with them. . . . People attending these ceremonies usually respond positively. It becomes a way to reach unbelievers since they have never seen anything like it. (185–86)

The Movement Has Inspired and Helped Start CPMs Among Other Unreached Groups

Only about 10 percent of known CPMs have started new CPMs in other unreached people and places. The Bhojpuri movement has reached that level. We have described that expansion in two chapters of the book: "Breakthrough Beyond the Bhojpuri" and "Breakthrough among Muslims" (121–55). This movement's impact on other groups has also been described in other publications (Coles and Parks 2019, 185–88). As of mid-2019, "About eight different language groups across Northern India have been impacted and those language groups have different sub-groups within them. The work in at least one of those has already reached the point where it can be called its own Church Planting Movement" (Coles 2019, 18).

The Movement Has Felt the Lord's Call to Let Many of Its Stories Be Told

The Indian context brings significant persecution. Yet, the movement's approach is both open enough and contextual enough that we decided to publish key stories and principles from the movement. This differs from many movements, which, because of safety concerns, don't allow their stories to be shared publicly. A case study of the Bhojpuri movement was first published in *Perspectives on the World Christian Movement* (Winter and Hawthorne 2009, 697–700). Descriptions of the movement have brought some criticism. Those are often reacting to a second-hand oral report rather than the written descriptions. We shared a response to some criticism in an interview published in *Mission Frontiers*:

> Dave: Sometimes people travel through an area where a movement has been reported and they don't see evidence of it, so they think there's no movement happening there. How would you respond to that?
>
> Victor: (laughs) You can walk in a jungle and never see any animals. That doesn't mean there are no animals in the jungle. Some people have a certain image in their minds of what a Church Planting Movement will look like. They think they'll see people crying in the streets, or shouting loudly that they're saved. They expect to see crosses on top of houses, and no more temples, mosques, or idols. They have this idea that when a movement happens, the area will look very Christian. . . . We don't have people streaming to church buildings on Sunday morning. Bhojpuri believers live, dress, and eat like other Bhojpuri people. They gather to worship in relatively quiet ways. (Coles 2019, 18)

Being willing to share the dynamics working in the Bhojpuri movement has helped many people better understand what is actually happening in this movement. This has also reduced some misunderstandings about CPMs in general.

What Leadership Features of the Movement Are Countercultural?

Power Dynamics

In Indian culture, those in power often prefer a system that keeps their power and limits the power of those they lead. This is also true in many other cultures and in many churches throughout history. The Bhojpuri movement has taken a different approach by focusing on empowering others instead of holding onto power.

> The movement avoids special religious titles. It empowers all believers to become leaders in their context, using their unique gifts. This way of leading is one of the keys to the ongoing growth of the movement. Everyone in the movement knows their leaders and who they lead, but leadership is really about serving rather than having a rank or title. (John and Coles 2019, xvii–xviii)

"Empowerment is a key part of our leadership training. We aim to empower leaders from day one" (164).

The culture of empowerment affects many parts of the movement. First, besides encouraging new believers to share the good news, we show them how to start new worshiping communities. We empower them to start new groups right away. We support and release these new disciples to lead the new groups they start. . . . Second, we empower grassroots leadership at the local level. We help local leaders start new worshiping communities. We don't set up work that depends on outsiders, which would make the work vulnerable. We empower local leaders. This brings local ownership, leading to long-term success and growth. Third, we empower and equip all believers to do ministry in Jesus' name. (176–77)

"The movement thrives because all of God's people are empowered to serve the Lord" (187). "Multiplication happens naturally when everyone takes ownership, feels empowered, and obeys God's commands" (199).

Kavilash, one of the longtime workers with the movement, shares:

If I compare the early days with now, many things are different, but some things have stayed the same. The work is now much bigger, but one thing didn't change: since the very beginning, there has never been pressure to bring results. The work is not focused on numbers, so we can work freely without any pressure. We serve because we are motivated from the heart. (14)

Women in Leadership

Indian society has traditionally held women in low esteem. The Bhojpuri movement, in strong contrast, holds women in high esteem and includes them in leadership.

Gender issues are a huge problem in North Indian society. Men and women treat each other differently after accepting Christ than they did before. They now show love and care that goes against all previous customs and traditions. Men and women share equal responsibility in sharing the good news and moving it forward. They also share equal responsibility in making disciples, leaders, and churches (45).

We see women as equal partners in the good news and in the ministry. This is against the usual culture and intentional on our part. From the very beginning, we have believed that men and women are equal. Just as God calls men, He calls women too. If men can make disciples, women can make disciples. So we have many women who are leaders and church planters in the movement. They have trained people and won whole families. We have no problem with appointing women as leaders in the church. The head of our organization is a woman, a wonderful servant leader. (196–97)

No Religious Titles

The movement does not use special religious titles. "This movement is built on non-traditional but very biblical patterns of leadership and leadership development. We don't use special church titles for leaders (Matt 23:8–11), and we equip and encourage all believers to minister, using the gifts God has given them (1 Pet 4:10–11)" (173). "We empower and equip all believers to do ministry in Jesus' name. This means no division between clergy and laity. We avoid thinking that leadership is about titles and don't call our staff 'Reverend' or 'Pastor'" (177). "Our avoidance of titles intimidates some people, but it works. It's both different and biblical" (158). "We just avoid the traditional Christian idea that important ministry should be linked with payment and a title" (177).

Overcoming Caste Challenges

In Indian society, the usual cultural pattern, which many expect, is that caste will be a deciding factor in one's success. This has not been the case in the movement. In fact, the movement has some low-caste people leading high-caste people.

> We have one low-caste woman who leads a worshiping community on the low-caste side of the village. Then she goes to the high-caste side of the village and leads another worshiping community there. Even though she comes from a low caste and is female (which makes her an unusual leader in any village), God is using her effectively in both the high-caste and low-caste areas. (25)

"Other Indians visiting with us were shocked she could do that. We learned that after she prayed for healing for some high-caste people and God healed them, they didn't care what caste she came from. God's truth and power can break down any walls" (xii).

Literacy Not Required for Leadership

"We believe that leadership should not depend on education or status. Our movement includes some leaders who are not literate at all" (172). "Leaders also need to make sure the entire church planting process is . . . doable. . . . If the process is simple, educated people can do it as well as those who are not. But if it's complicated, only a few experts can do it" (118).

Learning Christian leadership is usually an academic process. In the early days, most Bhojpuri leaders had little education. It would have been a disaster to try traditional Christian leadership training. Most of them learn by listening. Some of them have a few years of schooling. However, their ability to learn comes mainly through listening, not reading.

To do things the Western way, a person must be able to read to be trained as a disciple, leader, mentor, or church planter. . . . We aimed to keep it simple: focus on prayer and sharing the gospel and simple learning of Scripture, used in daily life (160–61).

Kavilash shares:

> When I first got involved with the Bhojpuri work, I was not very educated. I had only finished second grade. As I got involved in the movement, I began to get more educated—mostly not in regular school subjects, but in biblical education. Then I became eager to learn and I finished up to eighth grade in just a couple of years. I was most excited about the trainings we did because they helped me learn the Bible and understand it much better. (14)
>
> We worked with an illiterate woman who gained great recognition in her community. That happened through her work in the child literacy program, the sewing program, and the health awareness program. She takes pride in doing these things and shares, "I used to be a nobody, but because of this work I have become a somebody." (55)

Plurality in Leadership

Church leadership in the movement is usually shared by multiple people. This differs from Indian cultural norms and the pattern in many churches around the world. "Churches normally have several elders and multiple levels of leadership, not just one leader. When the church grows or when a leader is away, things work better with shared leadership" (184). This effort to follow the New Testament pattern has provided strength, stability, and repeatable growth in the Bhojpuri movement.

Conclusion

God's Spirit loves to work in unique ways, and his work in the Bhojpuri movement has been special in many ways. In both its leadership and how it has grown, the Bhojpuri CPM has created a unique path by God's grace.

References

Coles, Dave. 2019. "A Still Thriving Middle-Aged Movement: An Interview with Victor John." *Mission Frontiers* (May–June).

Coles, Dave, and Stan Parks. 2019. "DMM—Disciple Making Movement." In *24:14—A Testimony to All Peoples*. 24:14.

Dale, Tony, Dale Felicity, and George Barna. 2009. *The Rabbit and the Elephant: Why Small Is the New Big for Today's Church*. BarnaBooks.

John, Victor, with Dave Coles. 2019. *Bhojpuri Breakthrough: A Movement That Keeps Multiplying*. WIGTake Resources.

Narayan, Deepa. 2018. "India Is the Most Dangerous Country for Women." *The Guardian*, July 2. www.theguardian.com/commentisfree/2018/jul/02/india-most-dangerous-country-women-survey.

Winter, Ralph, and Steven Hawthorne. 2009. *Perspectives on the World Christian Movement: A Reader*. 4th ed. William Carey Library.

4

A Thai Multiplication Movement

Adapted by Stephen Bailey

The history of Christian missions among Southeast Asian Buddhists has been a discouraging one.[2] After roughly 350 years of Christian missions in Thailand, less than 1 percent of the population is Christian, and most Christians come from ethnic minority groups. Thai Christians are largely not from Buddhist Thai family backgrounds. Now, however, there has been a breakthrough in reaching Thai Buddhists for Christ. The Free in Jesus Christ Church Association (FJCCA), led by Pastor Somsak, is seeing many Thai Buddhists become Christians. Since 2017, 89,009 Thais have become Christians. Over 27,000 (30 percent) of these new believers have been baptized. In the process, the FJCCA has started 6,275 village churches and 49 district churches. They now have a total membership of 36,017 Thai Christians (Martin 2024).

This response to the gospel in Thailand is so new and unique that I went to see Pastor Somsak and meet his team at his home in Phetchabun Province in north central Thailand. The main office of the FJCCA is at Pastor Somsak's business in Chon Daen town in Phetchabun Province. He runs an oil change and car wash business, which also provides office space for the movement. Earlier in his life, Pastor Somsak successfully sold life insurance. Then, thirty years ago, God gave him a vision to plant what is now Chon Daen Church. Between 1987 and 2016, Pastor Somsak and the members of the Chon Daen Church planted thirteen more churches in Central and Northeast Thailand.

Later, in 2016, God gave Pastor Somsak a new vision to reach ten thousand new believers, and his church quickly met that goal. Now the

---

2 The Southeast Asian Theravada Buddhist nations are Cambodia, Laos, Myanmar, Sri Lanka, and Thailand.

FJCCA has taken on a much larger vision. The FJCCA came to understand that 95 percent of all the villages in Thailand had yet to hear the gospel. This led them to set a goal of sharing the gospel in every village in the country. They began planting churches in villages all over Phetchabun, Phichit, and Nakhon Sawan Provinces. Today, every village in these three provinces has a village house church and a larger district church. (Every province consists of several smaller districts.) Their new goal is to plant a house church in every village in the four provinces of Khon Kaen, Chaiyaphum, Phitsanulok, and Kamphaeng Phet.

During my time with the FJCCA team in Phetchabun, I observed a steady flow of Buddhist-background Thais deciding to follow Jesus. I tried to understand why this was happening so easily through this ministry. Of course, the big reason is that God is doing something new in Thailand. But it is also worth trying to understand how God is using Thai Christians to reach their Buddhist neighbors today.

One of the first things I noticed was the large number of lay Christians who volunteer their time to share their faith and teach the Bible to new believers in the villages. About 70 percent of these volunteers are women. Pastor Somsak also works with a software engineer named Dwight Martin to keep track of all the new believers and house churches. This helps them stay organized and follow up quickly with all the new Christians.

The FJCCA team also does some interesting things to help Buddhists understand the gospel. For instance, they realized that the Thai word for God (*Prachao*) can cause confusion. This word can refer to many kinds of gods and even spirits. To avoid this confusion, the FJCCA has chosen to only talk to the people about Jesus (*PhraYesu*). Talking about Jesus rather than a generic god (*Prachao*) helps Thai Buddhists understand that the gospel is about the God named Jesus.

The FJCCA teams each have five or more volunteer church planters. They begin by finding "a person of peace"—a person in the village who is open to hearing the gospel. They ask this person to introduce them to their relatives and friends in the village who might be interested in hearing the gospel. They also ask permission from the village headman to hold a small meeting to share the gospel with the villagers.

The evangelism meetings take place outdoors so everyone passing by can hear. The event may be as small as ten or twelve people, or as large

150 or more. Most young people and men have left the villages to work in cities or other countries. So, the village gatherings consist mainly of adult women, elderly retired men, and children.

The volunteer teams follow Thai cultural rules carefully. They make the meetings fun, respect the elders, and share food with everyone. Everyone who attends receives a bowl of noodle soup served by smiling volunteers. They invite everyone to participate and often play a game. The team members know how to be polite and show respect to local authorities and elders. The team shares their testimonies with enthusiasm and confidence, as well as a simple Bible lesson. The team communicates a simple and clear gospel message with stories illustrated with poster pictures. Then, two or three people share their testimonies, explaining why they follow Jesus. The last speaker asks if anyone would like to pray to Jesus for needs in their life. Almost every hand goes up. Before the team finishes, they ask if anyone would like to ask Jesus to enter their heart and stay with them. Those who want to accept Jesus are led by the team in prayer to receive Jesus into their lives.

Reciting prayers aloud and in unison is a traditional Buddhist temple practice familiar to everyone. New believers are encouraged to pray the prayers on their own and develop their own relationship with Jesus. They are taught that they can pray anytime. To empower them to do this, they receive a paper with five short prayers printed in a large font. The prayers are for morning, noon, and evening, confession, and times of need. The large font is important in villages since many of the elderly have poor eyesight and homes with poor lighting. The children have their own meeting and are led through a short, simple explanation of the gospel.

During these village evangelism events, typically ten or more adults show a desire to follow Jesus. The majority of converts are married, middle-aged, relatively poor village women. From this core of new believers, a house church is formed. Every week, one or more volunteers from the team return to the village to teach the new believers. Team members return until a leader is raised up from within the house church. New believers attend the house church until they have grown in their faith. They have the option to attend a mother church on Sunday in a district town if they desire. However, this is not encouraged at the beginning of their walk with Jesus.

The FJCCA plants churches in clusters as the gospel moves from village to village through neighbors and friends. When they have twenty to thirty house churches in an area, they find land and build a one-room district church building. This building will be large enough to hold one hundred to five hundred people. They construct a kitchen area behind the church building to serve church fellowship meals. The district church serves as a central worship center and training center to strengthen the surrounding house churches. In this way, training, resources, and encouragement are made available to house churches in the area.

A district church service follows a typical contemporary Thai Protestant order of service. It consists of a welcome, announcements, singing of worship choruses, receiving an offering, and a sermon. The only unique part is that three to five people share what they learned from the Scriptures during the past week and how their life in Jesus is different from their old life. This practice is common in their house church gatherings as well.

The first few months of a new believer's Christian faith are an important time in their spiritual lives. Typical Christian church services are very different from Buddhist temple ceremonies. The experience of going directly into a typical church can overwhelm a new believer from a Buddhist background. For this reason, new believers are encouraged to remain in their village house church for the first six months. Once they have grown in their knowledge and confidence in their new faith, they decide where they will worship. Many choose to attend both the village house church and the district church.

New believers also decide when they want to be baptized. This can happen right after they identify themselves as Christians or much later. They are taught that being baptized indicates a person has decided to abandon their former objects of worship and Buddhist ceremonies. At that point they are ready to worship only Jesus. The spiritual and social transformation of poor village women into confident disciples of Jesus can easily be observed in their testimonies and eagerness to volunteer their time and food to take the gospel to the next village.

The FJCCA movement has several interesting characteristics. One of the most interesting is that they do not forbid new believers from going to a Buddhist temple or fulfilling their obligation to help family members make merit. Instead, the FJCCA leaders leave the decision to end participation in these Buddhist practices up to the new believer. It seems to work best to give new Buddhist-background believers time to assure their family members of their love and respect. It is also best to let them decide when and how they will stop participating in the temple ceremonies. This often requires multiple discussions with family members. The FJCCA leaders have observed that new believers navigate this issue as they grow in their knowledge of the Christian faith. When the time is right, new believers stop their involvement at the Buddhist temple and ask to be baptized.

At one church, I met the lay Buddhist leader from the temple directly across the street from the church. He explained that he was a new believer in Jesus, but he still leads the Buddhist congregation through the temple merit-making ceremonies. He explained that the villagers had asked him to continue until he is able to find a replacement, even though they know he is a Christian. This kind of easy accommodation to the needs of both is common among Thai people but not typical in Protestant churches. This practice of giving new believers a transition period preserves the new believer's relationships with their family and friends.

In the past, many Thai Buddhists who have become Christians have returned to Buddhism after a short time. This usually happens because their families cannot accept their decision to follow Jesus and end their involvement in the Buddhist merit-making ceremonies. Because the FJCCA team allows new Christians to transition slowly to full allegiance to Jesus, they can find a way to show honor and respect to their families. This protects good relationships at home and encourages their relatives to consider becoming followers of Jesus. This helps us understand why a high percentage of new believers in this movement continue in their faith.

Conversion in this movement is a process. It includes praying that Jesus will take away their bad karma, asking Jesus to come into their lives, being discipled, becoming a member of a house church, learning to follow and pray only to Jesus (rather than to other gods), turning over household temple ceremony duties to other family members, and, when they feel ready, public baptism.

Another interesting characteristic of the FJCCA is that none of their leaders have any formal Bible or theological training. The movement is led completely by lay volunteers, the majority of whom have not been Christians for long. This is significant in light of the history of church movements, which have almost always had a high involvement of lay people. Those who are new in their faith often feel more comfortable and serve more effectively in non-church, missional contexts because they come from those contexts. Missionary professor Ralph Winter once said, "Most missionaries are and always have been lay people. I refer especially to the women missionaries" (1993). Many of the great missionaries in history have been lay people. The famous missionary to China, John Nevius, described the ideal missionary church planting team this way:

> Believers stay in their own professions; unpaid lay leaders shepherd the churches; churches meet in homes or simple structures; missionaries and paid evangelists oversee several churches, give extensive training; churches plant daughter churches. (Visser 2008, 51)

In one village that the FJCCA team took me to, I met a woman who has led hundreds of people to faith in Jesus. She makes and sells noodle soup for a living. When she isn't doing that, she travels on a small-engine motorcycle to other villages, sharing the gospel and doing discipleship. The FJCCA movement has many lay people like her. New believers in Thailand are excited to be involved in sharing the gospel and starting new village house churches.

We can cite another reason why, in the past, new believers have not continued in their faith in Thailand. There has often been a lack of follow-up to guide new believers into mature Christian lives. Discipleship involves a lot of work, but the FJCCA has many volunteers and a digital tracking system. So, they can quickly and consistently follow up with each new believer. The FJCCA pays careful attention to the discipleship process in two important ways. First, they follow up with new believers within forty-eight hours. The teams carefully record the new believer's name, address, the date they came to faith, age, gender, etc. They enter this data and the person's photograph into a database that tracks new believers and the location of all their house churches.

Second, new believers are discipled in an easy-to-understand, step-by-step process. Initially, a new believer is given a small booklet called *Jesus' Plan for Us* (printed in a large font). This helps the person better understand the gospel. Each lesson is reviewed and taught again in their community meetings, and new believers are encouraged to practice teaching the lesson to others as well. This eventually results in believers having a firm grasp of the gospel and the ability to articulate their new faith. Later, new believers enter a second level of discipleship that introduces them to the Gospel of John through a book called *The Water of Life*. A third book, *Abundant Life*, covers basic doctrine. The third level of discipleship guides new believers in reading and studying the Bible in their house church.

Pastor Somsak has given the FJCCA teams a practical and flexible approach to ministry. They constantly evaluate their ministry and make adjustments to improve it. They are open to using any method that facilitates the rapid and easy spread of the gospel, helping people understand the gospel easily and feel at home in the church. They discard anything that becomes an obstacle to the spread of the gospel.

In one village we visited, the gospel presentation was delayed because it rained so hard that no one could hear, even with the public address system. Because the rain did not let up for a long time, some of the audience left. When the team later tried to hold the event, the audience was small and did not pay attention. Afterward, the team discussed what to do next time. They decided to plan a fun activity for the group to do while waiting for the rain to stop. They hoped this would keep the audience's interest and help them hear the gospel.

Another factor that helps the FJCCA movement is the good roads that allow volunteers to ride their motorbikes into remote villages. Also, everyone in Thailand has a cellphone. This helps them coordinate worship and teaching times for remote village churches.

A third factor that supports this movement is that Thai people, as a nation, feel discouraged right now. Not long ago their beloved king died. In 2014 the military took over the government, and there are few jobs in the countryside. At the same time, some Thai people are less committed to Buddhism than in the past. All these factors have created an openness in the hearts of Thai people to hear the gospel.

I asked Pastor Somsak about the potential for religious persecution in response to the rapid growth of their churches. After all, if this movement continues to spread throughout the country, some Thai Buddhists might feel angry about it. At least for now, Pastor Somsak feels confident this will not happen. Thailand has always been open to other religions and religious freedom.

During my first day with Pastor Somsak, he twice looked at me and said, "It's easy to win the Thai for Christ." I found this statement surprising. But as I watched him and the team, I saw they had an effective way of communicating the gospel to Thai villagers in their area.

Something unique is happening in Thailand today through the FJCCA movement. For the first time in more than 350 years of missionary work, significant numbers of Buddhists are choosing to follow Jesus. The FJCCA method of sharing the gospel and planting village churches makes sense to Thai people. As a result, thousands of people are now following Jesus. The movement is learning and adapting as it grows. This movement is flourishing, not only because many Thai people are becoming Christians but also because many of these new believers are sharing their faith with their family and friends. As a result, small house churches are being planted in thousands of villages for the first time. God is on the move in Thailand!

References

Martin, Dwight. 2024. "Christmas Update from the Martins in Thailand." Personal Newsletter. December 2024.

Visser, Marten. 2008. "Conversion Growth of Protestant Churches in Thailand." PhD Diss., University of Utrecht. Missiological Research in the Netherlands 47.

Winter, Ralph. 1993. "Missiological Education for Lay People." *International Journal of Frontier Missions* 10, no. 2 (1993): 75–81.

PART 2

How Shall We Understand What's Happening?

5

Discipleship Movements Today
A Primer from Multiple Perspectives

Warrick Farah

The world's population grew four times larger in the twentieth century. Christianity kept up with this growth, staying around 30 percent of the global population. The church has become smaller in the Global North and has grown significantly in the Global South. However, while tens of thousands of Muslims come to faith in Christ each year, another 35.5 million Muslims are born. Tens of thousands compared to millions.

The situation is similar among Hindus and even worse among Buddhists. The world's unevangelized population grows by about seventy thousand people every day (Johnson and Zurlo 2019). The hard truth for those who want to see Jesus worshiped in all nations is that the world is getting more "unreached" each year (Parks 2017).

At the same time, the "movement" paradigm has become an important trend in the evangelical missions community. Articles, books, and training events about movements keep appearing in various mission groups. Mission agencies have big dreams. In 2018, an initiative was launched to get people to pray that 10 percent of the Muslim world would be reached in the next ten years. Sometimes it feels like everyone is talking about movements. Researchers have found nearly two thousand movements to Christ that include more than 115 million believers.[3] According to Long (2020), most of them are in places that previously had no church.

We should pause and reflect during all this action. What really are these movements? How can we better understand movements, both in all their complexity and as a specific way to do ministry?

---

3 2414now.net/resources.

I have outlined a study of movements, sometimes called church planting movements (CPM) or disciple making movements (DMM), in a previous article (Farah 2020). In this chapter, I want to go deeper. I will briefly introduce movements from the views of church history, church structure, sociology, and mission practice. I aim to create a framework for thinking critically about movements today.

1. A Historical Perspective

Christianity can be described in many ways, but it is a movement by nature. As a worldwide movement, it is the largest and most successful movement in history. Jesus started with twelve disciples (Luke 6:12–16) and sent out seventy others (Luke 10:1–24). On Pentecost, three thousand people believed and were baptized (Acts 2:41). The numbers kept growing every day (Acts 2:47). What began as a Jewish movement soon spread to gentile (non-Jewish) areas as the apostles changed their ministry approaches (Acts 15; 1 Cor 9:21). In Acts 19:10, we read that "all the Jews and Greeks who lived in the province of Asia heard the word of the Lord" while Paul was in Ephesus for two years. As Andrew Walls says, "Crossing cultural boundaries has been the life blood of historic Christianity" (2002, 32). The mission "to the ends of the earth" (Acts 1:8) has crossed many barriers and become "home" for more cultures than any other movement.

Multiplication in the Early Church

In the parable of the soils, Jesus teaches that the "word of God" would grow a lot in some places, up to a hundredfold (Luke 8:4–8, 11–15). In Acts, Luke often uses words like "greatly" (6:7), "daily" (16:5), and "mightily" (19:20) to show how quickly the early church grew. "Luke clearly tries to show the amazing and widespread spread of the gospel to fulfill the kingdom-growth theme in the Gospels" (Ott 2019, 112).

Acts and Paul's letters show local movements of Jesus followers who gathered in house churches. "Rather than a strategy for spreading the gospel, the CPMs in Acts were the result of faithful followers of Jesus empowered by movement leaders to make more disciples, who gathered together in the homes of believers" (Cooper 2020, 19). In other words, movements were not a plan but the result of a passion for Jesus shown by making disciples.

In his letter to the Romans, Paul said there was "no more place for me to work" (15:23) from Jerusalem to Illyricum (now Albania). Craig Ott comments that Paul could confidently say he had "fulfilled the ministry of the gospel of Christ" (15:19 ESV) only if he believed that the churches he had started would keep growing and finish the work he began. "There is simply no other way to explain the dramatic numeric growth and spread of Christianity during the first centuries" (2019, 114).

By the year AD 300, there were 6.3 million Christians in the Roman Empire (Stark 1996, 7).[4] The church did not focus on speed but on more leaders equipping more believers for more ministry (Eph 4:11–12). Paul commanded believers to pray "that the message of the Lord may spread rapidly and be honored, just as it was with you" (2 Thess 3:1). This seems to be a biblical pattern for New Testament Christianity: "a balance between evangelistic urgency and healthy growth" (Ott and Wilson 2010, 77).

Yet we can also see that the early Christian movement was not exactly a "CPM" as some CPM experts describe today. The early Jesus movement did not become what we would call the Christian church until around AD 200 (Jenkins 2018). The movements in the second century were still quite varied. They included many "Christian" groups that were later condemned as heretical by early church councils. They also changed with the times, including sporadic persecutions and epidemics in the Roman Empire.

While faithful house churches read the biblical Gospels and Letters, the twenty-seven-book New Testament was not officially accepted until the end of the fourth century. In the second and third centuries, this "movement" did not grow mainly through organized evangelism and church growth plans. It grew through a Christlike, different way of life—patience during suffering and persecution. Christian movements have not always stayed in one place; they often shrink and sometimes even disappear. The overall movement of Christianity is one of repeated, not steady, growth (Walls 2002, 67).

Movement Ethos in Contemporary Missiology

Given this, how did the movement idea start to be included in modern missionary strategies and goals? A generation after William Carey went to

---

4 Cooper estimates around 5.5 million (2020, 32). Both writers think this was about 10 percent of the total population. Some believe this percentage was enough to influence the greater society (Xie et al. 2011; Cooper 2020, 29).

India in 1793, mission societies struggled with managing new churches in many non-Christian areas that had been set up outside of "Christendom." Mission leaders Rufus Anderson and Henry Venn usually get credit for the "three-self" formula. This meant that independent local churches, not foreign mission societies, would themselves become the way to spread missions in the world. This three-self formula taught that churches should be self-supporting, self-propagating, and self-governing. In other words, they should be free from colonial influence and dependence.

John Nevius took and taught this different approach to ministry in Korea in 1890. He added that Christians should stay in their social groups before converting. Also, that there should be a discipleship program based on regular Bible study. After this teaching, which started the Christian movement in Korea, the three-self formula became known as the Nevius method. However, the traditional "mission station approach" continued in many places.

In the early twentieth century, Roland Allen further developed the Nevius method in his famous book *Missionary Methods: St. Paul's or Ours?* (1912). Allen urged his peers to move away from traditional methods and focus clearly on biblical principles that led to local churches. At the same time, many people were coming to faith in some places. Waskom described this in his book *Christian Mass Movements in India* (1933).

Paul Hiebert says these mass movements of conversions had lasting effects in both church formation and community change. "Pickett found that not only were people's lives transformed, but also their decisions were reinforced by their new Christian community. Individuals were not torn out of their social networks. Rather, whole communities were changed" (2008, 328).

Pickett also greatly influenced Donald McGavran, the father of the church growth movement. McGavran took Pickett's ideas further into a theory he called "people movements." This was also based on observing phenomena. McGavran also highlighted how group connections help start or limit movements. In his book *The Bridges of God*, McGavran tried to answer, "How do groups of people, not just individuals, but families, tribes, and castes, become Christian?" (1955, 1). He also created the "homogeneous unit principle" (HUP), which says, "People like to become Christians without crossing racial, language, or class barriers" ([1970] 1990, 163).

René Padilla criticized the HUP as going against the example of Jesus and the apostles. He said it doesn't take the ministry of reconciliation seriously and has "no biblical foundation" (1982, 29). However, the issue seems to be that people should be able to worship God in their own culture and not be forced into foreign expressions of the faith. Local responses to the gospel will create different cultural expressions of church. These are both valid and necessary for the growth of world Christianity. In other words, the diverse nature of the church is not a threat to biblical faith. Rather, it shows Christianity's very nature of continuity. McGavran's observation is further balanced by the fact that while movements may start in the same ethnic or language group, they rarely stop there. As mentioned earlier, Christianity as a movement is known for crossing boundaries and uniting diversity (Acts 11:20; 13:1; Gal 3:28).

In recent years, leaders like Bill Smith, Victor John (2019), David Watson (2014), and Ying and Grace Kai and Steve Smith (2011) have built on these strategies. The resulting movements have yielded an incredible number of churches planted and communities changed. Today, researchers, like David Garrison through his books *Church Planting Movements* and *A Wind in the House of Islam*, have documented the rise of movements in the Global South. According to Garrison, "No one remembers who first used the term 'Church Planting Movements,' though it seems to be a change of Donald McGavran's important 'People Movements' to emphasize the unique aspect of creating multiplying local churches" (2011, 9).

In my view, CPMs differ from people movements. People movements are often linked with favorable social and political conditions that help them happen. CPMs might be better called "lay-led small-group discipling movements." The small groups themselves grow and multiply (at least up to four generations) and often in social networks. This can happen with or without good social and political factors. The main driver of the CPM process tends to be easy-to-copy churches with group interactive Bible study as their main practice.

Motus Dei by Nature

The Bible and church history show that Christianity, by nature, is a movement (and much more than a movement). Indeed, "No people group or nation has become identified with Christ without a movement happening among them at some point" (Lewis 2020, 8). Faithful disciples grew in the first three centuries without complex evangelism plans, and their growth led to more churches. The modern missions era, between 1800 and 2000, saw a huge growth of Christianity in the Global South. Meanwhile, the end of the twentieth century saw the church shrinking in the West. These factors greatly renewed interest in studying biblical faith as a movement of God (*motus Dei*).

Biblical faith is indeed *motus Dei* by nature. This must lead to studying things that might inhibit movement in current theology. Are there unbiblical teachings and traditions that need to be unlearned because they're stopping movements? With that question in mind, we might need to relearn six themes in discipleship movements:

1. An immediate relationship with Jesus through the Holy Spirit, which empowers "ordinary" believers for ministry
2. A willingness among leaders to innovate
3. An emphasis on biblical principles for missionary methods
4. The phenomenon of multi-individual conversions within social networks
5. The central role of Bible study in making disciples
6. The local ownership of churches, independent from outside control or help

We now take a closer look at this issue of church structure.

2. An Ecclesiological Perspective

Theologian Howard Snyder reminds us, "The Bible doesn't give a clear definition of 'church.' Instead, it gives many different images" (2010, 1).

Paul Minear describes ninety-six New Testament images for the church ([1960] 2004). Minear's four "master images" are:

1. The people of God
2. The new creation
3. The fellowship of faith
4. The body of Christ

Each of these images has appeared at different times and places throughout history. While no church is perfect, a mature understanding of the church should include all the biblical themes into the "mystery" of the church.

Ecclesiology Anchored in Deep Theological Identity

This mystery includes the diverse nature of biblical church structure. Movement theorist Alan Hirsch notes that "church structure ... is the most flexible of the core doctrines" of Scripture (2016, 143). Changes happened in the New Testament church whenever its organization hindered the spread of the gospel and the formation of churches.

Church structure is best understood not by defining its functions, but by having a strong theological identity that allows new forms of church. As Jesus was sent into the world, so are we (John 20:21). Since the church is the sent body of Jesus, the church's identity is missional by nature—meaning sent into the world.

Adaptive Ecclesiology in Christian, Post-Christian, and Non-Christian Contexts

Biblical church structure had flexibility anchored in its theological identity. Yet most church structures limit their descriptions of the church to long-established *Christian contexts*. These tend to be led by pastors, focused on programs, and centered around buildings. We want to raise a more important question—about new church structures in *non-Christian contexts* (frontier settings). We need a church structure for places where there was no church before. One bridge to this gap in research is the "missional church" literature describing church structure in *post-Christian contexts*.

Michael Moynagh uses the term "new contextual churches" to describe Christian communities serving people mainly outside the church. They make disciples a priority and form a new church among the people they serve. Moynagh shows how the New Testament church worked through homes, and emerging house churches reflected the structures of their social context.

Ed Smither similarly notes this feature of early church structure:

> As the oikos [Greek for household] structure was a natural way for social networking in the ancient world and with the deliberate

focus by Jesus and Paul to minister from house to house, the house church model was central to mission strategy through the early fourth century. Even when we think about large Christian communities like those in Rome, Carthage, and Antioch, we must imagine a network of house churches. (2014, 154)

Thus, as the early Jewish church used a model similar to the synagogue, the early gentile church adapted to the Roman household, or *oikos* (e.g., Rom 16:5; 1 Cor 16:9; Col 4:15; Phlm 2). Depending on the context, new churches today in non-Christian settings will similarly adapt.

Multiplying Microchurches and Defining Church

The flexible house church, or "microchurch" model, seems essential for developing a movement church structure. Supporters of simple churches believe that the first-century church is the standard for today. They note that "primitive" church structures are most often found in movements (Snyder 2010, 10). Similarly, Michael Cooper concludes that "the New Testament shows the local nature of the church, and this, no doubt, helped the rapid growth of house churches throughout the Roman Empire" (2020, 184–85).

Alan Hirsch suggests that the body of Christ has the hidden potential for movement built into it, as the church is naturally movemental. However, the church's teachings, values, and structure often stop or limit that potential. According to Hirsch (2016, 78ff), the apostolic genius of New Testament church structure for sustaining movements is shown by six factors.

1. The absolute centrality of Jesus Christ
2. The priority of making disciples
3. A mission-focused, incarnational attitude toward the world
4. Leadership that can both start movements (apostles, prophets, evangelists) and sustain them (shepherds, teachers)
5. Natural systems instead of top-down organizations
6. An outward-focused, inclusive community that can take risks and thrive in them

This kind of "church as movement" structure differs from the "church as industrial complex" structure common in Christendom (Woodward and White Jr. 2016, 24). To regain the energy of the early church, the New Testament and the Holy Spirit must be the main sources for comparing traditional models with the church structure of CPMs.

Large, already existing churches and denominations can help start movements. Studies such as *Megachurch Christianity Reconsidered* (Gitau 2018) show how megachurches in the Global South provide stability for people in unstable urban areas. These are not simply copied from the West. These types of churches are growing in various urban centers. However, the movement church structure in CPMs is better described in smaller, flexible groups. Large, stable institutions might sometimes be needed to support smaller, more vulnerable churches in movements.

As mentioned before, the New Testament shows a flexible church structure. It doesn't give a clear definition of the church form. However, without some biblical standard, like Acts 2:42–47, the very idea of "church" becomes almost meaningless. J. D. Payne talks about the need for an irreducible minimum to define the church. A simple definition of a church is also helpful because adding extra requirements from outside the Bible can hinder local church growth.

Missiologist L. D. Waterman defines church as "a significant group of Jesus' followers having an identity as a church (*ekklēsia*) who gather together regularly on an ongoing basis, with recognized leadership under the headship of Christ, to worship God and encourage one another in obeying all his commands (including, but not limited to, baptism and the Lord's Supper)" (2011, 467).

Simple definitions tend to focus on the *functions* of the church, not necessarily its *theological identity*. The irreducible minimum church structure requires that a group of believers in Jesus starts to call themselves "a church." They also try to learn and obey Scripture, practice baptism and communion, have recognized spiritual leaders, and see their spiritual unity with other Jesus followers. However, discipleship groups that eventually become biblical churches do not do so overnight. A mature church assumes mature disciples. Especially in movements, younger church forms often take time to grow into churches.

Toward a Movemental Ecclesiology on the Frontiers

In summary, most church structures describe the church either in Christian or post-Christian areas. No unique church idea has been described for Africa or Asia. We need more development of church in non-Christian areas, especially for church movements. (See Larsen's helpful chapter in this volume.) One key element of movement church structure includes focusing on the early New Testament forms of church. These also grew in non-Christian areas and proved to be reproducible. As we have seen, the New Testament church:

1. Was mainly made up of flexible microchurches or house church networks
2. Matched the structure of its cultural and social setting
3. Was led by apostles, prophets, and evangelists, as well as by shepherds and teachers (Eph 4:11), not just pastors like today's church
4. Saw itself as a mission-focused community of Jesus followers created by the Holy Spirit

Biblical churches such as these are most reproducible and also most common in discipleship movements today. Support and leadership from large institutions may provide healthy stability to smaller churches. However, traditional churches may often try to control smaller church groups that they assume are under their authority.

3. A Sociological Perspective

Because movements happen with groups of people, they can also be seen through the lens of sociology. Sociology explains how individuals become groups. With the right biblical understanding, social sciences help explain some of the means God uses to fulfill his purposes. We can see these means described in the Bible and in our world today. God works through social conditions to bring about faith in Jesus, and these conditions can be studied sociologically. This section introduces some basic sociological theory to view the dynamics of movements as the spread of faith across social networks.

Conversion, Social Networks, and the "Person of Peace"

Most studies of conversion have focused on the individual level. However, looking at the group level can provide more insights into what's happening. Many studies have shown that social networks have a large influence on religious communities. For example, social networks often play a bigger role than doctrine in bringing individuals into a faith community. Networks also act as the main way for spreading faith to a wider world.

Research has found the gospel's spread through natural social networks linked with planting more churches. Individuals have the personal choice to follow Jesus. At the same time, their social network strongly influences them in ways they often don't realize.

One important idea in movements has been the "person of peace" (Matt 10:11; Luke 10:5–6). In CPM/DMM literature, this person acts as a gateway into a community or social network. Jerry Trousdale writes that "people of peace are God's pre-positioned agents to bridge the gospel to their family, their friends, or their workplace" (2012, 90). However, some debate whether the Bible clearly teaches the person of peace idea. Descriptions of a person of peace differ, and some worry that it could lead to an overly simple strategy for church planting (Matthews 2019). However, the person of peace principle has been well documented in the study of movements (Garrison 2004, 45, 213).

This principle matches a key part of social network theory, where social "brokers" act as bridges. When brokers fill the gaps between networks, they create change. These bridge people connect others together to spread new ideas into new networks. Whether or not it is a biblical principle, we can see it clearly in movement dynamics. It isn't wrong to look for such people.

The "Right Set of Circumstances" and Social Structure

Christians believe the ultimate source of effective ministry is the Holy Spirit. But we can compare ministry to a sailboat prepared to sail. We can ask, "Is my ministry positioned to move the way he blows so that it can become a movement of God?" (Smith 2013, 29). We may also ask if movements can happen in *any* context, if the Holy Spirit moves and our ministries are correctly positioned. Clearly, many people and places are resistant to Christian ministry of any kind. Social scientists often talk about social movements needing the right set of circumstances. Movements are helped by having the right leader with the right innovation in the right place at the right time. Successful movements often spread in the middle of an unpredictable and complex mix of conditions. It's almost impossible to predict the tipping points, when movements start to grow quickly. We can best understand them *after* they happen.

For example, most documented movements today are found in rural, developing areas in the Global South. They consist of simple churches. Most happen in societies where extended families are largely intact. People don't already deal with multiple identities or belong to many groups.

Thus, movements seem to be limited by one or two things:

1. hierarchical or institutional church structures; and/or
2. urban and complex modern societies.

However, several movements in Asia exist in cities (e.g., Kai and Kai 2018, Kindle 151; John and Coles 2019, chap. 8). These movements are usually not citywide. They thrive within ethnic neighborhoods or small parts of cities. In fact, several movements that started in rural areas have moved into city neighborhoods as the people moved.

This raises more questions about where movements are most likely to happen:

- Are movements limited in the individualistic West by the breakdown of household structures?
- Has the West been inoculated to movements by the decline of Christendom?
- Does the rationalistic, Enlightenment worldview in the West hinder the supernatural elements often common in movements?
- What role does private media play in secular individualism?

Little research has been done on these types of social and cultural issues. We still have much to learn. But clearly both context and situation matter. And the unpredictable movement of the Holy Spirit is the ultimate deciding factor (John 3:8).

Discovery Bible Study, Ritual, and Energy

Movements involve a lot of energy from people who join and advance the movement. Movements both create energy and require energy from participants. One tool that does this in many discipleship movements is Discovery Bible Study (DBS). DBS and abundant prayer act as symbols of group membership in DMM strategy.

DBS and group prayer are interactive. They focus on inductive learning and active participation. Regular DBS keeps people moving toward situations that provide emotional energy. The Holy Spirit inspires disciples as they practice New Testament ways of following Jesus, who is actively working in the community. Movements have a social expectation that everyone is responsible for the ministry, not just the leaders.

Non-Christian religions have no formal equivalent of DBS. This may be why DBS, along with group prayer and fasting, and local worship music, create positive experiences for new believers. The Holy Spirit creates new and exciting energy through group interaction around the living and active word of God (Heb 4:12). The early church gatherings also seemed to be very participatory (1 Cor 14:26–33). Genuine discipleship movements involve a deep, personal spirituality around the gospel.

Obedience-Based Discipleship and "Strictness"

Successful movements grow because energy turns into action from participants. Especially for discipleship movements, the DMM/T4T strategy prioritizes obedience-based discipleship over knowledge-based discipleship. Obedience-based discipleship started as a counter to the rational focus on mere knowledge found in much Western discipleship. In this model, obeying biblical commands like evangelism and godly behavior is preferred over merely cognitive "discipleship" focused on passing on information. Accountability in obedience creates an environment where following Jesus brings serious life transformation. The Watsons note, "Modern church has made the Christian life too easy for its members" (2014, 39). Jesus's combination of high challenge and high invitation for his followers is essential for creating missional movements. This combination trains Christians to be active producers, not passive consumers, of their faith.

A well-known sociological paradox says, "Religions that demand the most from their members often grow the fastest, but as religions become large and successful, they tend to become less strict" (Conley 2011, 583). It may not seem logical for people to join a community that demands a lot from them. However, strict churches are often strong because they have high levels of commitment. Strictness also reduces the number of "free riders" who contribute little to the community and thus lower the overall level of participation and enthusiasm. As movements grow, they need to maintain accountability, knowledge, and faithfulness in a healthy balance.

Identity and Insiderness

Andrew Walls has said that throughout history, followers of Jesus tend to be naturally "at home" in their context and, at the same time, "pilgrims" (1996). This reflects the Bible's paradox: being in the world, but not of the world (John 17:15–18). This tension describes how movements grow within each different context. New believers find a balance of being inside the context in some way ("in the world") but also outside in some way ("not of the world").

Without downplaying the belief aspects of a religion, sociologist Robert Montgomery says that "people will be receptive to or resist a new religion according to whether they perceive that it enhances or detracts from an aspect of their social identities which they value" (2012, 268). Places that are more resistant to the gospel are likely places where biblical faith is seen negatively. Meanwhile, places that have experienced large movements have seen the newness of faith in Jesus as positive.

Movements relate to their contexts in different ways; insiderness is not the same for everyone. Movements also change over time, and the way they relate to their context changes. We also need to distinguish so-called "Insider Movements" from CPM. They are not the same. However, issues of identity and insiderness play a crucial role in helping or hindering movements. In many different ways, movements happen within their context and are not seen as just foreign imports from the outside.

The next section will give an overview of movements from the view of mission practice.

4. A Practical Perspective

A weakness is a strength overused. Many applications of movement mission studies are biblical and inspiring. But movement leaders and movement theory itself can become unbalanced by overusing strengths. This may also happen when mission workers with little experience misuse movement approaches. This section will point out a few overuses of movement mission studies. These are sometimes done by new Western missionaries who might lack good mentorship or a well-rounded understanding.

Activism and Patience

Movements involve a lot of activity that can be described as activism. Movement leaders should be admired for their determination and courage. In times of political chaos and natural disasters, practitioners often help those suffering. Also, leadership training for movement leaders often includes evaluation of what leaders need to do at different stages of movement. Activism is one of the core skills of Jesus's followers (2 Tim 4:5).

However, mature movement leaders understand that activism must be balanced by theological reflection. We must always ask, "What is happening behind what is happening? What does the Bible say about what I am doing right now?" Questions such as these create godly patience and a dependence on the Holy Spirit.

Activism can also lead to a task-focused ministry, ignoring hurting people who might not be people of peace or people of influence. For Jesus, the original movement leader, no one was invisible. The marginalized in society seemed especially important to him. Movements tend to minister effectively to the oppressed in society. Finally, activism can lead to an unhealthy type of practicality. Of course, there are biblical reasons for certain kinds of practicality (1 Cor 9:19–23). Experienced movement leaders know that an activism that focuses on tasks over relationships and practicality over theology is corrected by a patient trust and thoughtful understanding that ultimately the movement belongs to God, not to us (Ps 46:10).

Obedience and Grace-Filled Holistic Spiritual Formation

Biblically speaking, the discipleship process affects the whole person. This brings notable changes in beliefs, actions, and emotions. As mentioned earlier, obedience-based discipleship focuses on the behavioral part. Correct belief (orthodoxy) is clearly important, but obedience reminds believers of the importance of correct actions (orthopraxy) in making disciples. The Bible also talks about the need for correct feelings (orthopathy) for complete spiritual growth.

Obedience works in an environment of grace and wholeness where the gospel is the basis for all discipleship and mission.

Patterns and Contextualization

Many movement strategies provide a clear roadmap for leaders to follow in their disciple-making ministries. DMM, T4T, Four Fields, and others like them offer a simple pattern of goals and action points that many leaders have found helpful. These strategies can be misunderstood as being formulas. However, experienced leaders understand the importance of context. No two movements are the same. When we look closely at movements, we can see great diversity reflecting local applications of biblical faith. Movement strategies have a strength in simplicity that more complex strategies lack. Movement strategies have given leaders tools for starting and growing that earlier less-defined approaches lacked.

Simple Methods and Strong Theological Training of Leaders

One of movements' great strengths is their development of leaders. This normally happens through on-the-job training. Training leaders while they are doing ministry is much more effective than classroom training. Movements develop leaders using methods similar to Jesus's methods. These include following, experiencing, and doing. Movement leaders (especially in DMM) often lead with the Bible open in the DBS process. Movements are often Bible focused rather than leader focused, especially in oral societies. God's word and the lordship of Jesus are "the parallel paths guiding the movement" (Garrison 2004, 182).

Yet DBS and frequent Bible studies do not substitute for (formal or informal) theological training. DBS alone does not encourage the types of analytical thinking leaders need for handling complex issues in their context. More depth is needed for strong local theologizing to happen.

While DBS focuses on areas where theological training is lacking, the reverse is also true. The issue is not balance but integration. Movement leaders integrate on-the-job leadership development with deeper theological training for leaders. This does not mean that leaders also need an official degree or ordination. Movements and theological training are not opposed. As disciples pursue faith seeking understanding, faith comes first.

Conclusion

Some ways of making disciples are better suited to movements than others. Yet this doesn't mean that context is unimportant or that traditional church structure is wrong. It also doesn't mean that bigger is better or that numbers necessarily prove success. The standard for ministry is always the revelation of Jesus Christ. True discipleship movements only happen when Jesus is the focus.

Movements are an exciting reality in God's world today. They show promise for changing lives and communities in all nations. Movements offer a way to see biblical transformation happen on a much larger scale than traditional approaches. At the same time, we need to keep learning and equip people for critical thinking. This is essential for our changing world and God's diverse mission.

Movements invite the combination of historical, theological, sociological, and practical research. As participants in God's movement, we need to better understand how movements are happening and how they can be supported more effectively.

Our goal is to learn more about how God is working in our world. We want to apply this knowledge well, both in what is taught and training those wanting to support movements today.

References

Allen, Roland. 1912. *Missionary Methods: St. Paul's or Ours?* R. Scott.

Conley, Dalton. 2011. *You May Ask Yourself: An Introduction to Thinking Like a Sociologist.* 2nd ed. W. W. Norton.

Cooper, Michael T. 2020. *Ephesiology: The Study of the Ephesian Movement.* William Carey Publishing.

Farah, Warrick. 2020. "Motus Dei: Disciple-Making Movements and the Mission of God." *Global Missiology* 2 (17): 1–10.

Garrison, David. 2004. *Church Planting Movements: How God Is Redeeming a Lost World.* WIGTake Resources.

Garrison, David. 2011. "10 Church Planting Movement FAQs." *Mission Frontiers* 33, no. 2: 9–11.

Garrison, David. 2014. *A Wind in the House of Islam: How God Is Drawing Muslims Around the World to Faith in Jesus Christ.* WIGTake Resources.

Gitau, Wanjiru M. 2018. *Megachurch Christianity Reconsidered: Millennials and Social Change in African Perspective.* IVP Academic.

Gitau, Wanjiru M. 2008. *Transforming Worldviews: An Anthropological Understanding of How People Change.* Baker Academic.

Hirsch, Alan. 2016. *The Forgotten Ways: Reactivating Apostolic Movements.* 2nd ed. Brazos.

Jenkins, Philip. 2018. "When the Jesus Movement Became the Christian Church." The Anxious Bench, March 9, 2018. https://www.patheos.com/blogs/anxiousbench/2018/03/end-beginning-jesus-movement-became-christian-church/.

John, Victor, and Dave Coles. 2019. *Bhojpuri Breakthrough: A Movement That Keeps Multiplying*. WIGTake Resources.

Johnson, Todd M., and Gina A. Zurlo, eds. 2019. "Status of Global Christianity, 2020, in the Context of 1900–2050." World Christian Database. https://www.gordonconwell.edu/center-for-global-christianity/wp-content/uploads/sites/13/2020/02/Status-of-Global-Christianity-2020.pdf.

Lewis, Rebecca. 2020. "Patterns in Long-Lasting Movements." *Mission Frontiers* 42, no. 3: 8–11.

Long, Justin. 2020. "1% of the World: A Macroanalysis of 1,369 Movements to Christ." *Mission Frontiers* 42, no. 6: 37–42.

McGavran, Donald. 1955. *Bridges of God: A Study in the Strategy of Missions*. Wipf & Stock.

McGavran, Donald. 1990. *Understanding Church Growth*. Eerdmans.

Minear, Paul S. 2004. *Images of the Church in the New Testament*. 2nd ed. Presbyterian Publishing.

Montgomery, Robert L. 2012. *Why Religions Spread: The Expansion of Buddhism, Christianity, and Islam with Implications for Missions*. 2nd ed. Cross Lines Publishing.

Moynagh, Michael. 2014. *Church for Every Context: An Introduction to Theology and Practice*. SCM.

Ott, Craig. 2019. *The Church on Mission: A Biblical Vision for Transformation Among All People*. Baker Academic.

Ott, Craig, and Gene Wilson. 2010. *Global Church Planting: Biblical Principles and Best Practices for Multiplication*. Baker Academic.

Parks, Kent. 2017. "Finishing the Remaining 29% of World Evangelization." Lausanne Global Analysis 6, no. 3.

Payne, J. D. 2009. *Discovering Church Planting: An Introduction to the Whats, Whys, and Hows of Global Church Planting*. InterVarsity Press.

Shenk, Wilbert R. 1981. "Rufus Anderson and Henry Venn: A Special Relationship?" *International Bulletin of Missionary Research* 5, no. 4: 168–72. https://doi.org/10.1177/239693938100500404.

Smith, Steve. 2011. *T4T: A Discipleship Re-revolution*. WIGTake Resources.

Smith, Steve. 2013. "CPM Essentials on a Napkin." *Mission Frontiers* 35, no. 6: 29–32.

Smither, Edward L. 2014. *Mission in the Early Church: Themes and Reflections*. James Clarke.

Snyder, Howard A. 2010. "Models of Church and Mission: A Survey." Center for the Study of World Christian Revitalization Movements. Edinburgh, UK.

Stark, Rodney. 1996. *The Rise of Christianity: A Sociologist Reconsiders History*. Princeton University Press.

Trousdale, Jerry. 2012. *Miraculous Movements: How Hundreds of Thousands of Muslims Are Falling in Love with Jesus*. Thomas Nelson.

Van Engen, Charles. 2000. "Church." In *Evangelical Dictionary of World Missions*, edited by A. Scott Moreau. Baker Academic.

Van Gelder, Craig. 2000. *The Essence of the Church: A Community Created by the Spirit*. Baker Books.

Van Gelder, Craig, and Dwight J. Zscheile. 2011. *The Missional Church in Perspective: Mapping Trends and Shaping the Conversation*. Baker Academic.

Walls, Andrew. 1996. "The Gospel as Prisoner and Liberator of Culture." In *The Missionary Movement in Christian History: Studies in the Transmission of the Faith*. Orbis.

Walls, Andrew. 2002. *The Cross-Cultural Process in Christian History: Studies in the Transmission and Appropriation of Faith*. Orbis.

Waterman, L. D. 2011. "What Is Church? From Surveying Scripture to Applying in Culture." *Evangelical Missions Quarterly* 47, no. 4: 460–67.

Watson, David, and Paul Watson. 2014. *Contagious Disciple Making: Leading Others on a Journey of Discovery*. Nashville: Thomas Nelson.

Xie, J., S. Sreenivasan, G. Korniss, W. Zhang, C. Lim, and B. K. Szymanski. 2011. "Social Consensus through the Influence of Committed Minorities." *Physical Review* E 84, no. 1.

6

"The Word of the Lord Spread Through the Whole Region"

The Book of Acts and Church Planting Movements

Craig Ott

Protestants and evangelicals are often called "people of the Bible." It makes sense for us to examine church and mission practices by comparing them to what the Bible says. Church Planting Movements (CPMs) and related strategies have been closely studied, and people have reached very different conclusions about them. Some praise these movements, while others criticize them harshly. These movements are dramatic and unlike anything seen since the early days of Christianity. They focus on simple, repeatable methods that allow local believers to lead new churches without depending too much on missionaries, outside funding, or formal training. CPMs are controversial, and people tend to have strong opinions about them—both for and against. The main question we'll explore in this chapter is: What does the Bible, especially the book of Acts, have to say that applies to these movements?

This chapter will not try to prove or disprove CPM strategies or look at specific methods, such as Discovery Bible Study (DBS). Instead, we will look at examples in Acts where the message of Jesus spread quickly, churches started and grew, and whole regions were reached with the gospel. From these examples, we will try to identify principles that could guide CPM strategies today. We will start by discussing how we should read Acts and apply its lessons today. Then we'll look at specific cases from Acts and reflect on what those stories teach us about CPMs.

Reading and Applying the Book of Acts Today

Some people argue that missiologists (people who study missions) don't always base their strategies on the Bible. They claim that instead of starting with biblical teaching, missiologists observe what God is doing in the world and then look for Bible verses to justify the strategies bringing those results. While this approach can sometimes be done in a shallow way, we can see a similar approach in Acts. Leaders observed what was happening and then tried to view those events in light of Scripture. For example, the apostles didn't fully understand at first how God was including gentiles in his plan. This new understanding created conflict in the early church, which wasn't resolved until seventeen years later at the Jerusalem Council (Acts 15). At that meeting, the apostles and elders looked back at how God was working, reexamined Old Testament teachings, and figured out what that meant for the growing movement of Jesus followers.

It's not a good idea to try to find a Bible verse to support every single mission strategy or method. However, it is wise to think about modern movements in light of biblical principles. Instead of asking if modern CPMs are identical to what we see in Acts, we should ask if they are consistent with the direction and theology of Acts. For this reason, this chapter focuses less on methods and more on the dynamics of how the gospel spread and how churches were planted, as described in Acts.

The Purpose of Acts

To understand Acts, we need to understand why Luke wrote it. Scholars have debated Luke's purpose, but it seems most likely that he wrote primarily for gentile Christians. He wanted to provide a reliable history of the early church and to show how the gospel spread widely through the power of the Holy Spirit. A major theme in Acts is the inclusion of gentiles in God's plan. The frequent mention of the church's growth shows God fulfilling his promise to bring salvation, light, and blessing to *all* nations.

Acts focuses more on the work of the Holy Spirit in spreading the gospel than on specific strategies or methods. The book is full of stories about how the gospel spread to new places and how it overcame different kinds of challenges. Paul is featured as the main missionary to the gentiles, but Acts also highlights how the message of Jesus reached marginalized and unexpected groups, building on themes introduced in Luke's Gospel.

Principles over Methods in Acts

Instead of looking for specific methods in Acts, we should focus on the underlying principles. This frees us from trying to rigidly copy what happened in Acts. Luke didn't write Acts as a how-to manual for missions or church planting. Instead, he focused on the Holy Spirit's role in guiding and empowering the early church.

This means we don't have to test every modern mission strategy by asking, "Do we see this exact method in the Bible?" Instead, we can think about how to apply the larger story and principles of Acts to our modern context. We need to remember that as Paul did his ministry, the New Testament did not yet exist. Our world today is different from the world of the first century. So, while some events in Acts are unique to the early days of the church, the general principles—like relying on the Holy Spirit and adapting to different cultural settings—still apply.

Church Planting Movements in Acts?

Some critics of CPMs argue that movements like this don't appear in the Bible. It's true that Acts doesn't describe a CPM as we define it today—hundreds or thousands of churches, in at least four generations of churches—multiplying rapidly in a few years. However, Acts does describe movements of rapid growth and expansion, and we can learn from those examples.

Passages throughout Acts (2:47; 5:13-14; 6:1, 7; 9:31; 11:21, 24, 26; 12:24; 13:49; 14:21; 16:5; 19:10, 20) mention significant growth. We see phrases like "daily" (2:47; 16:5), "rapidly," a "large number" (6:7), and an increase in "great" numbers (11:21, 24, 26; 14:1). Whole regions were impacted by the gospel (9:31; 19:10; 13:49). These descriptions suggest that many people became believers and churches formed in many local areas.

This kind of growth could only happen if believers, leaders, and churches were being reproduced. The idea of multiplication is central to CPM strategies, and we see this concept described in Acts as significant. The language of "being fruitful and multiplying" (Gen 1:22) appears in the Bible as a way of describing how God's people grow and fill the earth with God's glory. Jesus builds on this idea in the kingdom parables. Kingdom growth in Luke's Gospel continues in the church's growth as Luke describes it in his second volume, Acts. We also see Paul instructing Timothy to train leaders who will train others in multiple generations (2 Tim 2:2). 1 Thessalonians 1:8 also shows that Paul considered it normal for churches to reproduce and evangelize their region. The multiplication of disciples, leaders, and churches is an important theme in Acts.

The Church in Jerusalem

The Jerusalem church started on the day of Pentecost when the Holy Spirit came and Peter preached to a large crowd. About three thousand people believed and were baptized that day (Acts 2:41). Despite opposition, the church kept growing to five thousand and later to "many thousands" (Acts 4:4; 21:20).

Although the Jerusalem church is unique in some ways, it shows that rapid, Spirit-led growth is possible. Fast growth does not imply a weak gospel message or shallow faith in the new believers. Luke emphasizes that while humans proclaimed the gospel message, it was God who added new believers to the community (Acts 2:47). This reminds us that church growth depends on God's work, not just human effort. Luke also links the continued rapid growth of the Jerusalem church to resolving conflict among the disciples (Acts 6:1–7). We see that believers' unity and addressing problems that arise are vital for a movement to keep growing healthy and strong.

Judea, Samaria, and Antioch

In Acts 8, we see that the gospel spread from Jerusalem to nearby regions because of persecution. Ordinary believers who were scattered shared the gospel wherever they went (Acts 8:4). In Antioch, a church formed when believers shared the gospel with gentiles, and "a great number" believed (Acts 11:21–26).

We should notice three things about this gospel spread. First, we see no mention of sending out evangelists or missionaries at that time. The gospel was proclaimed by "those who had been scattered" by persecution. Second, Jesus's scattered followers naturally shared the gospel wherever they went. As fairly new believers, they assumed they should share the good news with everyone. Third, the messengers were "ordinary" believers (not the apostles—Acts 8:1), empowered by the Spirit. Fourth, it was this young church in Antioch that the Spirit called to send out the first intentional missionaries (Acts 13:1–3). The young churches honored their connection with the older Jerusalem church (Acts 11:27–30; 15), but the gospel spread rapidly without waiting for a word from Jerusalem.

Pisidian Antioch

On Paul and Barnabas's first missionary journey, "The word of the Lord spread through the whole region" of Pisidian Antioch (13:49). This region included over fifty villages. So, the gospel's spread clearly didn't happen just because of Paul and Barnabas. Local (new) believers also helped spread the word, resulting in many more people coming to faith and house churches forming.

Because many people accepted the gospel, the local Jewish leaders got upset and forced Paul and Barnabas to leave town (13:50–51). But despite this opposition, "the disciples were filled with joy and with the Holy Spirit" (v. 52).

Later, Paul and Barnabas returned to encourage the new believers and appoint elders in the churches (14:21–23). Paul visited these churches several times to strengthen them. Appointing and encouraging local leaders was important for the churches' health and growth, even though in that setting the new leaders were fairly new believers themselves.

Later, in places having more mature believers around, the pattern for choosing church leaders became stricter, as seen in the Pastoral Epistles. But at the beginning of the movement, fairly new believers could serve as leaders.

Ephesus

Paul spent two years teaching in Ephesus, and during that time, "all the Jews and Greeks who lived in the province of Asia heard the word of the Lord" (Acts 19:10). Ephesus became a center for training and equipping leaders who carried the gospel to other cities. Note, this all happened within a two-year period! It's the New Testament's clearest case of church growth resulting in an entire province hearing the gospel and churches reproducing.

Acts 19:19 reports that the new believers burned their magic scrolls, publicly showing that they were leaving their old ways behind. This act of commitment had two results: increased opposition and increased spread of the gospel. Verse 20 reports that, "In this way the word of the Lord spread widely and grew in power." Those last words show both the quantity and quality of the movement. Its rapid impact went both wide and deep.

Acts 20:13–25 describes Paul's parting message to the elders of the church in Ephesus. This message shows his concern for the ongoing health and leadership of the church. The later warning in Revelation 2:1–7 reminds us that even a powerful movement is not guaranteed to stay strong.

Biblical Principles of Church Planting Movements

From Acts, we can see that rapidly growing movements were part of the early Christian experience. These movements spread the gospel across entire regions and led to the planting of many new churches. They challenge the idea that rapid growth is always shallow or unhealthy. They also hold open the possibility that similar movements can still happen.

We don't want to copy specific methods described in Acts. Instead, we want to understand the key ideas that can help us create and grow new movements in our time. While not everything in Acts applies directly to today, we can learn seven principles that can guide church planting movements (CPMs).

1. Movements Are a Work of God

Church planting movements depend entirely on God. The Holy Spirit gives power to the message and the messengers, as God brings people into the church. Paul wrote, "I planted the seed, Apollos watered it, but God has been making it grow" (1 Cor 3:6).

Although methods and strategies are important, they don't guarantee success. God works through obedient humans, but the growth of any fruit depends on his blessing. This is why prayer and trusting in God must always be the foundation of any mission strategy. Jesus made this clear when he said, "Remain in me, and I will remain in you. No branch can bear fruit by itself; it must remain in the vine" (John 15:4).

Signs and wonders—miracles, healings, and exorcisms—often accompanied the spread of the gospel in Acts. These acts of power confirmed the message and showed that God's kingdom was advancing. In our time, CPMs sometimes report similar miracles, which remind us of God's active role. However, the Bible warns us not to focus too much on miracles. They are not the goal but a sign of God's power and sometimes a door-opener for the gospel.

2. Movements Are Built on God's Message—the Gospel

In Acts, the growth of the church is closely tied to the spread of the "word of the Lord." The message of Jesus's death, resurrection, and salvation was preached everywhere. This message is the heart of church planting movements.

Paul and other apostles adapted the way they shared the gospel depending on their audience. For example, Paul used different approaches when speaking to Jews in synagogues and gentiles in public squares. However, the core message of the gospel never changed. Gospel messengers should never remove the offense of the cross but rather seek to make clear the meaning of the cross. Present-day CPM strategies also emphasize sharing the gospel in ways that fit the culture while staying true to the Bible. In every culture, the gospel calls people to reject all forms of idolatry, stop sinning, and accept the risen Christ as their Lord and Savior.

Paul preached and taught in public, and also from house to house (Acts 20:20). The Bereans showed noble character by checking the Scripture for themselves (17:11). They wanted to see if what Paul said was true. Early in Paul's travels he did not stay long in most locations. However, he taught for a year and a half in Corinth (18:11) and for three years in Ephesus (20:31).

The Bible is central to disciple making movements (DMM), one approach leading to CPMs. They rely on DBS, in which each person answers questions about the meaning and personal application of Bible stories. Paul told Timothy and Titus not to neglect the ministry of teaching. CPMs also need ongoing clear biblical teaching to prevent misunderstandings or false beliefs.

3. Movements Result from Evangelism That Includes Church Planting

When people became followers of Jesus in Acts, they joined local groups of believers (Acts 2:41, 47). These groups often met in homes, forming small churches. Nearly everywhere the gospel was preached, new churches were started.

Church planting is closely connected to evangelism. As more people come to faith, they need local churches where they can grow and worship together. DBS groups aim to become small churches as people come to faith. These churches might not look like typical Western churches with buildings and paid pastors. Instead, they might meet in homes and have leaders who are new believers. Yet, they still have the basic qualities of the churches described in Acts, such as teaching, fellowship, prayer, and worship.

4. Movements Empower Ordinary Believers to Share Their Faith

Acts shows that the gospel spread not just through apostles like Peter and Paul but also through everyday Christians. For example, after persecution scattered believers from Jerusalem, they shared the gospel wherever they went (Acts 8:4).

The important church in Antioch was started by unnamed believers who shared the gospel with gentiles (Acts 11:19–21). This shows that ordinary Christians (such as Epaphras—Col 1:7; 4:12), not just trained missionaries, played a large role in the early church's growth. The same pattern has been repeated throughout Christian history. Local disciples effectively spread the gospel to others.

We see the same pattern in CPMs today. Local believers share their faith, plant churches, and lead others to Jesus. While challenges may arise, the Holy Spirit works through ordinary people to advance the gospel.

5. Movements Depend on Local Leaders

While ordinary believers are essential to CPMs, the Bible also shows the importance of equipping strong local leaders. In Acts, Paul and Barnabas appointed leaders (elders) in the churches they planted. Paul considered leaders essential to the ongoing life of a church (Titus 1:5). These leaders were sometimes new believers, but Paul and Barnabas trusted the Holy Spirit to guide and strengthen them (Acts 14:23).

As movements grow, developing leaders becomes even more important. And as the believers mature, the standards for leaders are raised, as seen in Paul's letters to Timothy and Titus. The ongoing health of CPMs depends on equipping local leaders who can teach sound doctrine, protect against false teaching, promote spiritual life, and continue patterns of outreach.

6. Movements Can Expect to Face Opposition

Opposition is a normal part of following Jesus. Jesus himself warned that his followers would face persecution (John 15:20). However, Acts shows that the gospel often spreads even more during times of hardship. Every example of church growth in Acts involves some form of opposition.

Acts 4:4, 13:48, 17:34, and 18:8 all describe gospel advance directly after describing such resistance. The opposition came from religious leaders, governments, and even local communities.

Paul faced riots, imprisonment, and other hardships, but he never stopped preaching the gospel. He described the conflict this way: "For our struggle is not against flesh and blood, but against the rulers, against the authorities, against the powers of this dark world and against the spiritual forces of evil in the heavenly realms" (Eph 6:12). In the midst of such opposition, we see that the gospel progressed, churches were established, and effective ministry took place.

Movements today often face great opposition as well. Even when acting wisely and presenting the gospel in ways that fit the local context, wisdom should always be exercised; opposition still happens. This is predicted in Matthew 5:11–12, John 15:20, and 2 Timothy 3:12. Yet we can praise God that even amid severe opposition, the gospel is advancing by his power, according to his plan.

7. Movements Should Be Connected to the Larger Body of Christ

In Acts, churches weren't isolated from one another. They stayed connected through communication, support, and shared decision-making. For example, the Jerusalem Council brought leaders from different churches together to address important issues (Acts 15).

Paul often visited churches to encourage them and sent coworkers like Timothy and Titus to help them grow. Churches also supported one another financially, as seen in the collection for the church in Jerusalem. These connections helped create unity and shared purpose among the early churches.

Today, CPMs should also find ways to stay connected with the body of Christ—regionally and globally. Networking with other churches provides encouragement, accountability, and opportunities for partnership in reaching the lost.

Conclusion

Acts doesn't give us a step-by-step guide for church planting, but it does show us important principles that can guide CPMs today. We should invest our efforts in approaches that seem most likely to bear fruit. Not all methods are equally effective, and no one method will work well everywhere. We can thank God for ongoing research to discern the best means. At the same time, we know that humans cannot produce movements just by using a particular method. God must give the growth. CPMs will only emerge by his grace and in his timing.

Acts ends without a clear conclusion, leaving the story open for us to continue. As followers of Jesus, we are called to carry on the mission of spreading the gospel to all nations. Will the disciples we make, the churches we plant, and the movements that emerge reflect the same Spirit-led growth and discipleship found in Acts? That is the challenge before us today.

7

God's Expanding Family
The Social Architecture of Ekklēsia Movements

Trevor Larsen

The number of movements to Christ around the world has grown dramatically since 2006.[5] As these young movements get bigger and stronger, they face the challenge of becoming "*ekklēsia* movements." I use the word *ekklēsia* (Greek for "church") to mean groups of believers who follow patterns similar to those in the New Testament, not the patterns common in most modern churches.[6] These movements fit well in their cultures and consist of disciples making disciples while connecting them to communities of God's growing family. This chapter focuses on movements among unreached people groups (UPGs), which must survive and grow in tough conditions.

In this chapter, I will look at how ekklēsia movements today are similar to those in the New Testament. I will first explore some biblical patterns of ekklēsia movements during New Testament times, then explain how some current movements among UPGs show those patterns. The New Testament stages of ekklēsia, such as the early phase before Pentecost and the birth, childhood, young adult, and adult phases, give us good ways to think about these movements over time. I hope to show that developing ekklēsia from their beginning to full maturity is important for the new movements happening around the world today.

---

5 I use the definition of "movement" upon which many organizations have agreed: four or more generations of believer communities of more than one thousand believers within a limited number of years.

6 "Many of the churches planted by Paul would not meet what many today might consider a minimal standard for being an established church. Nevertheless, he addressed even the most problematical congregations as 'the church.' This forces us to consider more carefully what genuinely constitutes a local church in the biblical sense" (Ott and Wilson 2010, 4).

Hermeneutical Lenses for New Testament Ekklēsia Movements

To study ekklēsia movements, we need to answer these questions:

1. What parts of the New Testament talk about ekklēsia movements?
2. What are the contexts and growth stages of ekklēsia in those parts?
3. What authority do these biblical descriptions have for developing ekklēsia movements today?

To answer these questions, I will use three ways of understanding the Bible (hermeneutical lenses).

First Lens: The Jesus Band

The first way to understand ekklēsia in its early stage is the Jesus band, shown in the Gospels and Jesus's teachings. This lens includes five elements found in Jesus's ministry.

First, Jesus's original community of believers started by him telling people, "Follow me." Those who followed Jesus joined others who had done the same.

Second, Jesus presented a mission-focused vision for his faith community. He taught his disciples to go to receptive families and villages to share the gospel. This approach brought the good news to families and then to entire villages.

Third, Jesus defined ekklēsia as the family of God (Matt 12:48–49). Renewed families linked together as a new family became the social structure of the fruit of sharing the gospel. Jesus trained his disciples to act like brothers and sisters, showing love and serving others. He redefined leaders as servants who cared for God's family.

Fourth, Jesus taught about ekklēsia as representing God's kingdom on earth. He gave believers the authority to change people and free them from darkness (Matt 16:18–20). When his people come together to pray for the renewal of a brother or sister, Christ the King is with them (Matt 18:15–20).

Fifth, Jesus described ekklēsia as a work in progress, like a building being constructed and plants growing through their attachment to Jesus. These are the main features of the Jesus band, the first community of believers.

Second Lens: Disciples' Communities of the Spirit

The second way to understand how the early ekklēsia grew in different cultures is to look at the Spirit's role, as shown in Acts. The Holy Spirit plays a central role in forming ekklēsia in Acts, sending apostolic agents to launch gospel expansion. The result of the gospel spread by the Spirit is ekklēsia. God made ekklēsia more diverse by spreading it from Jerusalem (Acts 1–7) to other people groups (Acts 8–12) and then to gentile regions (Acts 13–28). Patterns in each place show how ekklēsia expanded and adapted to new peoples and places. Apostolic agents connected different regional churches into a larger network.

Third Lens: Social Dynamics in Movements

The third way to understand ekklēsia is by looking at the social dynamics of movements, found in parts of the Epistles. These show the community's values, behaviors, and relationships that shaped ekklēsia.

Pattern Imitation

A key idea in all three lenses is "pattern imitation," as we see in Paul's statement in 1 Corinthians 11:1: "Follow me, as I follow Christ." Paul encouraged many churches and mission teams to imitate these patterns. This is important for ekklēsia movements to grow quickly. Teaching alone wouldn't keep up with the growth, so following these patterns helps spread ekklēsia movements effectively.

Seven Ekklēsia Movements in the New Testament

Apostolic agents spread the gospel and created at least seven growing ekklēsia movements in the New Testament era. As these movements grew in different areas, more churches and diverse believers joined, creating a family-like network.

1. Jerusalem Movement

On the day of Pentecost, the Jerusalem movement grew to three thousand people (Acts 2:41) and then to about twenty thousand believers in three years (Acts 4:4). By Acts 21:20, some experts estimate thirty thousand Jewish believers in Jerusalem, even after persecution caused many to leave (Acts 8:1).

2. Movement in Judea and Samaria

Jesus and his disciples had won many believers in Judea and Samaria. After Jesus's death, the movement in Judea and Samaria multiplied further (Acts 8).

3. Antioch Movement

Seven years after the Jerusalem movement began, Greek-speaking Jews who left their homeland after Stephen's death started a new movement (Acts 11:19–21). This movement spread to Cyprus, Phoenicia, Cyrene, and centered in Antioch. Jewish believers won many gentiles in Antioch, showing that the ekklēsia was growing beyond Judaism.

When the Jerusalem church heard the news, they paid special attention to the believers in Antioch. They sent Barnabas to help them grow for a full year. Barnabas invited Paul to join him, and together they made Antioch a mission center. From there, the movement spread to other areas. Mission teams traveled to and from Antioch seven times. We don't know the number of believers in this movement. However, we do know that many unnamed believers helped spread the gospel, leading to a significant increase in diversity. Greek-speaking, bicultural Jews played an important role in this expansion.

4. Galatia Movement

A fourth movement flourished around the Galatian Province in Pisidian Antioch, Iconium, Lystra, and Derbe. We don't know how many believers there were, but Acts 14:21 tells us there were many disciples in the city of Derbe. Acts 14:23 reports that within one year the preaching of the gospel, elders were appointed to each new church, anchoring fast growth and maturity. This ekklēsia movement started with Jews in the region but soon grew strong among gentiles.

5. Macedonia Movement

A fifth movement happened in the province of Macedonia, with churches first established in Philippi, Thessalonica, and Berea. Three years later, Paul praised the new believers in Thessalonica for their influence throughout the provinces of Macedonia and Achaia and beyond (1 Thess 1:7–8). Paul praised this movement for their transformed lives, which were a strong witness (1 Thess 1:3–4, 9–10; 3:2–5), and for imitating the movement in Judea in enduring suffering for the gospel (1 Thess 2:14; 2 Thess 1:3–4).

6. Asia Minor Movement

A sixth movement occurred in the province of Asia Minor, centered in Ephesus. After the Jews rejected Paul's attempts to reach them, Paul spent two years intensively discipling a small number of disciples. These disciples then spread the gospel widely "so that all the residents of Asia heard the word of the Lord, both Jews and Greeks" (Acts 19:9–10). Based on the large value of the magic books burned in Ephesus (Acts 19:19–20), we estimate over ten thousand believers near Ephesus alone after only two years.

7. Achaia Movement

The gospel multiplied believer groups in the province of Achaia, in Corinth and Athens.

The Nature of Ekklēsia: Spiritual Family and Expanding Organism

In Acts, ekklēsia is created by the Holy Spirit. The Spirit empowers apostolic agents (Acts 1:8; 4:31) and uses miracles to convince unbelievers (2:4–13). When the Spirit comes upon new believers, they join the community and help build ekklēsia (Acts 2:38–47). The Spirit also protects ekklēsia's purity (Acts 5:3, 9), empowers leaders (Acts 6:3), and guides apostolic agents to spread the gospel (Acts 8:29). The Epistles describe more on this theme; the Spirit gives gifts to ekklēsia members to build it while unifying it (1 Cor 12). The Spirit bears witness with our spirit that we are children of God (Rom 8:16).

Ekklēsia is also a social community built on renewed families. Believers are called "the household of faith" (Gal 6:10) and treated like family members (1 Thess 2:7–14). Ekklēsia is a living, growing organism, continuously adding more believers and expanding like a family. Jesus promised he is building his ekklēsia (Matt 16:18).

Living images illustrate how ekklēsia grows, lives, sustains itself, bears fruit, reproduces, and moves into new areas and peoples (Eph 2:21–22; 4:15–16). It grows through repeating patterns: The social units replicate themselves as larger and larger units of the same kind. In the Bible, ekklēsia has no buildings or limits in location; it has an organic structure.

Social Structures in Ekklēsia
That Support and Sustain Its Multiplication

Three social structures are important for ekklēsia movements today: (1) two interdependent wings of ekklēsia, (2) three levels of linked ekklēsia units, and (3) teams of leaders.

1. Two Interdependent Wings of the Body of Christ

Mission Teams drove the expansion by spreading the gospel (Acts 9:15; 13:1–3). Jesus modeled this with his disciples, sending them in pairs to share the gospel, heal, and free people from evil spirits. He trained his disciples in three stages. Each time, he showed them what to do and then sent them out to practice. Jesus taught them to look for "receptive households"—homes that welcomed their message. These homes became their base for ministry in new places (Luke 10:4–7). First, he sent the twelve disciples to share the gospel only with Jews (Matt 10:5–6). Next, he sent them to Jews and non-Jews (Luke 9). Then, he sent out seventy-two more disciples to new areas (Luke 10:1–11).

The Jesus band's pattern in the first stage was "mission pairs to receptive households." Jesus sent out teams of two. They stayed with people who accepted the message. These homes helped them spread the gospel. The team then followed the same pattern to expand from "receptive hosts to receptive villages."

Their approach sometimes included a third phase: "mission pair to transformed witness." Some people who believed right away began sharing the message themselves. For example, the Samaritan woman told her whole village (John 4:39). The man freed from demons preached in his region (Mark 5:19–20). And Zacchaeus shared with his family and friends (Luke 19:1–10). Each of these homes became a new center for spreading the gospel.

In Acts, Jesus's mission plan continued. For example, Peter shared with Cornelius and his household (Acts 10:44–48), and Paul and his team shared with Lydia and the Philippian jailer's households (Acts 16).

Mission teams usually started ekklēsia in new areas. After starting a church, they appointed local elders in every church—usually within a year (Acts 14:23). Mission teams also supported churches across regions—teaching, solving problems, training leaders, and helping local leaders mature (Acts 6, 15; 20:17–38; 1 Thess 3). In addition, they connected churches in different places. They visited in person, wrote letters, prayed, sent trusted people, and helped churches in need (Rom 16; Col 4; Phlm).

Local churches took care of new believers and spread the gospel nearby. Local elders guided the church and sometimes sent members to join mission teams. Some local believers—especially those who spoke more than one language or knew more than one culture—shared the gospel with new groups. Examples include Peter, Philip, Priscilla, and Aquila.

Leaders—like apostles, prophets, evangelists, and pastor-teachers—helped train all believers to serve and build the church (Eph 4:11-16). Most believers served their local churches, but some—like Timothy—traveled and joined mission teams.

2. Three Levels of Linked Family Networks

The term ekklēsia is used flexibly in the Bible to refer to three sizes or levels: house, city, and region. Ekklēsia as house church was the basic unit, usually five to twenty people meeting in homes. As these multiplied, a cluster of these groups was linked as a city ekklēsia, led by a team of elders. Multiple city ekklēsia shared identity with other cities as a regional ekklēsia, led by wider-span leadership teams. *House ekklēsia, linked in clusters, was the primary component of ekklēsia for the first two or three centuries.* Early house church gatherings included the word, bread-breaking, prayer, koinonia fellowship, and shared funds (Acts 2:41-47; 4:32-37).

Differences within city ekklēsia tested unity and pushed believers to clarify that oneness in Christ includes some differences. On some issues, all the house and city ekklēsia in a region acted together. For example, believers in Macedonia acted as one ekklēsia that contributed to the needs of the poor in Jerusalem (Rom 15:26), though there were multiple city churches in Macedonia (2 Cor 8:1). Ekklēsia in Samaria, Judea, Achaia, and Galilee each had a regional identity (Acts 9:31; Rom 15:26; 2 Cor 9:2). Each region contained many city ekklēsia (the churches of Galatia: 1 Cor 16:19; the churches of Judea: Gal 1:22). These three levels connected like a family network, allowing ekklēsia to grow and support each other across different regions.

3. Leadership Teams

Each city ekklēsia had a team of elders to lead and support the church. Transferring leadership from the mission team to local elders within one year was an established pattern for apostolic teams. Selecting teams of local elders ensures local leadership, supports leaders' growth, and frees the mission team to move to the next area with the gospel. The leaders model what should be imitated, give spiritual guidance, teach, and solve problems.

Biblical and Social Features of Ekklēsia Movements in UPGs Today

After describing New Testament ekklēsia movements, I want to talk about modern movements in UPGs that follow similar patterns. Over sixteen years, a movement in Asia grew to eighteen thousand believers in small groups within twenty-seven UPGs in one country. It also multiplied in two other countries. Five years later, this network of movements had multiplied to three hundred thousand believers in small groups. These groups were within fifty-eight UPGs in one country and eighteen UPGs in other countries.

Sixteen movement leaders have been discussing and applying these principles for many years. Most are Bible college graduates or have doctorates in theology. One is a Bible college president; three others are seminary professors. In a recent discussion, they asked me to emphasize two aspects of the nature of ekklēsia. They view ekklēsia as a "Spirit brotherhood" and an organic system, not just an organization.

Movements as "Spirit Brotherhood"

Ekklēsia is spiritual at its core, not merely social. Ekklēsia movements are from God and belong to him. We are only God's servants who participate in God's mission to build ekklēsia. God's Spirit supplies divine capacity to build up the body of Christ, and the Spirit unites us as brothers and sisters in Christ. Ekklēsia is a spiritual family formed by its head, Jesus Christ. These brotherhood bonds, created by the Spirit, link ekklēsia movements in unity.

Movements as Organic Systems

Ekklēsia is an organism, not an organization. It is a system, but an organic system. In ekklēsia movements, most members are active, and one out of every five believers is leading others. Ekklēsia movements mobilize believers to meet social and emotional needs as well as spiritual needs. Ekklēsia is a living organism that grows and bears fruit. The ekklēsia gatherings are organically self-reproducing. They are always expanding, not limited to certain buildings or certain regions.

Applying the Principles in Our Context

Over many years, sixteen movement catalysts, each having apostle-like gifting,[7] developed consensus on three principles.

1. Ekklēsia is a living organism with two interdependent wings: apostolic teams and multiple local believer communities.
2. Ekklēsia is an expanding network, linking God's family in houses, cities, and regions.
3. Both wings of ekklēsia are led by teams of leaders.

These emerged through much Bible discussion, field practice, and evaluation together.

This team works to create many house churches and connect them to form bigger networks. Each house church joins a "cluster church," which includes ten to fifteen house churches. Cluster churches then connect to a "small region church," made up of three or more clusters. Finally, these small region churches are joined to a "wide region church," which includes at least three small region churches.

The team focuses on helping small groups multiply and grow. These groups read the Bible together, pray, and help each other and their communities. They link house churches into clusters, each led by teams of local elders. Leaders are trained for each cluster church and each regional church to guide the growing groups of believers. As these movements grow, the leadership teams oversee more and more groups.

The foundation of this movement is the house church and cluster, which are key to spreading the kingdom in these areas. During the time of the New Testament, house churches were often limited to ten to twenty people, though some could fit up to forty. Today, in areas with safety concerns, house churches have five or six believers. Because of social pressure and persecution, these groups don't grow by adding new people to existing ones. Instead, they start new small groups and help them grow. In other places, gatherings are larger.

---

7 "Apostolic agents" are different from New Testament apostles. They do not receive revelation from God. They are like the New Testament apostles in that they proclaim the gospel where Christ is not known, in new UPGs. And like the apostles, they have influence across regions as they build the linked connections of ekklēsia.

Even though these house churches are smaller, they multiply into many generations of groups. This movement has seen groups multiply through twenty-three generations and leadership teams expand across seventeen generations. Developing leaders as quickly as new groups form is one of their biggest challenges and is a major focus of their work.

The second level of ekklēsia is the city ekklēsia. In ancient Rome, eight house churches came together to form one city ekklēsia, with around seventy-five believers. A team of elders led this cluster of groups for the entire city. Among UPGs, large gatherings often face problems, such as backlash and increased challenges. A cluster church, which connects ten to fifteen small groups, also has about fifty to seventy-five believers and is led by elders.

The elders are responsible for things like managing the cluster's funds, baptisms, sharing God's word, and overseeing the Lord's Supper. They also guide community projects and Bible studies that focus on obedience to God and develop new leaders. Cluster churches are growing strong in many UPGs. Sometimes, the whole cluster church meets, but only when the elders think it's a good idea. The groups build unity through face-to-face meetings of leaders, visiting each other, and working together on shared ministries.

Local leaders encourage group leaders to visit one another to build trust, especially because there's often deep suspicion in UPGs. As trust grows through these visits, leadership groups are created for the cluster. A mentor helps guide and train these leaders, using a list of training modules. This helps the leaders do a better job supporting the ekklēsia in their region.

As ekklēsia spreads into larger areas, it grows based on factors such as travel routes, language, religious differences, and trust among people. A step up from a cluster church is a small region church. For example, in Ephesus, the city leadership team helped guide the house churches around the area. In the same way, a small region leadership team mentors all the cluster churches in a nearby area—usually within about an hour's drive. This closeness allows them to plan together, solve problems more effectively, and build trust and love.

This movement uses "coaching circles," where three leaders ask questions and support another leader in solving their challenges. For example, in Acts 6, the elders of the small region ekklēsia in Jerusalem helped settle a disagreement about providing food for widows. More recently, when a movement leader was too sick to travel, the small region's elders came together to make decisions about how to handle a cluster leader who had been beaten and hospitalized. They also called their mentor for advice.

A wide region leadership team oversees larger areas, which could be two provinces, one province, or part of a province. It depends on how much the local leaders have helped groups grow. After a big earthquake, while the movement leader was stuck elsewhere, the wide region team organized believers in the ekklēsia network to help those affected by the disaster. By the time the leader arrived two days later, they had collected enough donations to equal five months of a carpenter's wages. The wide region leadership team had done their job as area leaders, helping connect the many house churches in the region with the house churches that needed help because of the disaster.

In Acts 15, the elders in Jerusalem met with mission team leaders to solve a disagreement together. In our UPG movements, a leadership team from different regions meets every three months for three days. During these meetings, they work together to handle challenges, study the Bible, and support each other like a close family. These meetings have been especially important during tough times, like when we faced persecution and the COVID-19 pandemic, which sadly caused many losses.

Since the mission team works across different regions, they connect their network of small groups and leaders. Together, they help distribute food to people in need, create jobs for those who are unemployed, fix broken economic systems, and assist families who are having trouble with their children's education. By addressing community needs, the movement continues to grow.

The way ekklēsia is organized makes it easy for its spiritual community to grow and mature. It also helps them expand as a connected family network into new areas and UPGs.

A Final Word

Paul praised the ekklēsia in Thessalonica for quickly growing and becoming a model for other movements. Although he had directly discipled them for only three weeks, they quickly followed his pattern. In this way they became a model imitated by ekklēsia movements in several provinces. Many movements in our time echo Paul's prayer request to the Thessalonians: "Pray for us that the message of the Lord may spread rapidly and be honored, just as it was with you" (2 Thess 3:1).

8

But Is It Right?

Answering Objections to CPM/DMM

Dave Coles

In recent decades, many great works have been reported under the names "Church Planting Movements" (CPM) and/or "Disciple Making Movements" (DMM). Responses to these reports have ranged from great excitement to significant theological and missiological objections. In reviewing many articles and other discussions on the subject, I found eight main types of objections to CPM and DMM concepts.

1. Rapid reproduction is never promised in Scripture and often results in shallow discipleship. Aiming for rapid growth may frustrate workers and tempt them to exaggerate numbers.
2. The CPM/DMM paradigm does not adequately include the biblical role of teaching by spiritually mature teachers.
3. CPMs leave open a door for false teaching because of inadequate theological training for leaders.
4. CPMs have inadequate ecclesiology. (Their "churches" may not be real churches.)
5. The "person of peace" strategy is not really taught in Matthew, Luke, or Acts.
6. Obedience-based discipleship is a dangerous paradigm. It runs the risk of bypassing grace and teaching legalism.
7. Discovery Bible Study (DBS) is not a biblical approach to evangelism. The biblical pattern is proclamation.
8. It is unwise and dangerous to have unbelievers studying the Bible without any mature Christian present to guide their study.

As I address each of these objections, I will use the broader term—CPM. This has been defined as "a multiplication of disciples making disciples, and leaders developing leaders, resulting in local churches (usually house churches) planting more churches. . . . When consistent, multiple-stream fourth-generation reproduction of churches happens, church planting has crossed a threshold to becoming a sustainable movement" (Coles and Parks 2019, 315).

DMM is sometimes used to mean the same as CPM, but it is better understood as one of several *processes leading toward* a CPM.[8] Since objections often use CPM and DMM in a similar way, my response will also minimize the difference between the two, using the broader term: CPM. God is also working in other movements to Christ (including some described in this book) that don't fit the above definitions of CPM or DMM. This chapter will focus only on CPMs/DMMs and objections aimed at those ideas.

Objection 1

Rapid reproduction is never promised in Scripture and often results in shallow discipleship. Aiming for rapid growth may frustrate workers and tempt them to exaggerate numbers.

This concern has four important parts. I will address each one.

First, "Rapid reproduction is never promised in Scripture." This is true. We do a disservice if we promise (or make people think) that if anyone just does the right activities, a quickly growing movement will happen. The promises in Bible passages like John 15:5–8 and Matthew 13:23 focus on abundant fruit more than fast fruit. Yet God's Spirit inspired Luke to write positively of rapid gospel fruit. "The number of disciples in Jerusalem increased rapidly, and a large number of priests became obedient to the faith" (Acts 6:7). The apostle Paul not only remembered rapid growth

---

8 DMM "focuses on disciples engaging the lost to find persons of peace who will gather their family or circle of influence, to begin a Discovery Group. This is an inductive group Bible study process from Creation to Christ, learning directly from God through his Scripture. The journey toward Christ usually takes several months. During this process, seekers are encouraged to obey what they learn and share the Bible stories with others. When possible, they start new Discovery Groups with their family or friends. At the end of this initial study process, new believers are baptized. They then begin a several-month Discovery Bible Study (DBS) church-planting phase during which they are formed into a church" (Coles and Parks 2019, 315–16). Other processes leading to CPM include T4T, Four Fields, and Zúme.

among the Thessalonians but also asked them to pray for rapid growth in other places too. "Pray for us that the message of the Lord may spread rapidly and be honored, just as it was with you" (2 Thess 3:1).

So, rapid reproduction comes to us not as a promise but as a positive value in New Testament kingdom growth. Whatever else we say about rapid reproduction, we should reflect the positive view shown by New Testament writers.

Second, "Rapid reproduction . . . often results in shallow discipleship." Shallow discipleship is a sad reality throughout Christian history and in many parts of the Christian world today. A few factors often cause poor discipleship. These include:

1. Weak initial commitment, with little or no connection to the lordship of Christ.
2. Profession of faith based on just agreeing with beliefs, rather than true repentance.
3. Holding on to old sinful habits or cultural practices that don't match biblical commands.
4. Not having a strong ongoing relationship with active and growing believers.

These factors have troubled the church in a variety of cultures and settings. Many disciple-makers easily overlook how one or more of these factors may have affected churches in their own area. Yet they see clearly how these factors impact some churches in the Majority World (the results of past missionary work). In most such cases, the rapid growth that led to shallow discipleship was not from rapid reproduction. It was not a situation of spiritual generations of disciples making disciples and churches making churches.

The cases of rapid growth leading to shallow discipleship usually involve first-generation believers and churches, reached in large numbers with poor discipleship. This often includes one or more of the problems mentioned above. Biological reproduction then produces second- and third-generation Christians with average discipleship similar to or less than the first generation. In contrast, rapid growth in a healthy movement produces disciples with a strong and spreading faith. This differs from the slow-growth discipleship most of us are used to.

CPMs usually have values that address each of the four factors mentioned above. Discipleship through inductive Bible study creates healthy long-term habits. These include regular study of God's word, obeying God's word, and growing together with others. This kind of discipleship also builds faith commitment based on a solid process of understanding important biblical truths. It also makes clear the need to turn from one's old life to embrace the new.

CPMs normally have some system for follow-up and discipleship. Many have detailed plans designed to give believers strong doctrinal foundations for their life in Christ. The rapid generational reproduction in movements happens naturally from healthy disciples making healthy disciples. As mentioned before, shallow disciples rarely reproduce (except biologically).

Third, "Targeting rapid growth may frustrate workers." Rapid growth is not and should not be a goal by itself. As Craig Ott writes, "Our concern is not so much for speed as for locally reproducible methods that in the long run can start a self-sustaining movement" (Ott and Wilson 2010, 99). The rapid multiplication seen in CPMs happens naturally from God blessing the use of the right means to make disciples and plant churches. These means usually include reaching groups rather than individuals, much prayer, and consistent evangelism by all believers. They also include involving all disciples in studying and applying God's word and empowering local leaders. Using these methods doesn't guarantee a resulting movement. God doesn't promise a direct cause and effect in these matters, and neither should we. But faithfully using the right methods invites God's Spirit to do the work that only he can do, according to the Father's good will.

Simple, low-cost methods can multiply much faster than methods that need a lot of resources. Using these and other CPM-focused patterns often naturally leads to rapid multiplication. In fact, though, the early stages of starting a CPM rarely happen quickly. Many years are often required to learn a new language and culture and find a person of peace. Investing in leaders and seeing a Discovery Group continue to the point of decisions for Christ also require time and patient effort. CPM principles are not a recipe for quick success.

CPMs multiply quickly, but not because they focus on speed. They focus on immediacy: immediately obeying the Lord's word, like Jesus's first disciples did when he called them. He said: "'Follow me, and I will make you become fishers of men.' And immediately they left their nets and followed him" (Mark 1:17–18 ESV). Disciples in CPMs often obey the Lord's word without delay or hesitation. This leads to quick life changes and rapid multiplication of believers and churches. In CPMs, this kind of Christianity is normal.

One mission leader said that CPM trainers caused people to have unrealistic expectations. However, CPM training usually encourages people to do their best to follow biblical patterns while knowing that only God decides whether and when a movement happens. As long as we don't promise fast growth, we don't need to fear disappointing workers. Prayer and effort toward a big, hopeful vision inspires more progress than a small, easy-to-reach vision. Jesus encourages faith that can move mountains. So, even if a big-vision ministry does not end up starting a movement, God is likely pleased with such faith, prayer, and effort.

Fourth, "Targeting rapid growth may... tempt [workers] to exaggerate numbers." The temptation to exaggerate numbers exists among all workers around the world. This is true no matter what approach workers use in their ministry—CPM, traditional, or otherwise. This problem is greatest any time funding is connected to reported numbers. This includes arrangements where donors in a Western country send funds to support a "national" church planter. Although there are exceptions, CPMs generally avoid using outside funds to pay church planters. Many CPMs try to prevent reporting problems by using independent verifiers. For example, they might ask when groups meet and then make surprise visits.

Objection 2

The CPM/DMM paradigm does not adequately include the biblical role of teaching by spiritually mature teachers.

To address this concern, we first need to ask how God would have us measure what makes "adequate" teaching by spiritually mature teachers. I suggest that the adequacy of biblical teaching can be measured by these five factors:

1. Are people coming to true saving faith?
2. Are people growing as disciples, rooted and established in Christ?

3. Does the teaching lead people to obey everything Jesus commanded?
4. Does the teaching raise up leaders equipped to teach others? (This provides a strong foundation for generational growth and multiplication.)
5. Are the churches becoming healthy, biblical *ekklēsia*?

Trusted people have investigated many of the CPMs recognized by the 24:14 Coalition (www.2414now.net). Answers to these five questions have been positive. The teaching is adequate if the results are solidly biblical. Yet a few questions remain.

Do Movements Have a Role for Teaching by Spiritually Mature Teachers?

Yes, especially for teaching believers. Many CPMs have intensive teaching of new believers and leaders at all levels. For example, when asked, "What is the role of teaching and preaching in the movement?" Bhojpuri movement leaders said, "Teaching and preaching of the Word is a regular part of the believers' gatherings. Teaching also happens every month in the advanced leadership training, which gets passed on through the generations of the movement. Conferences and seminars also include teaching and preaching" (John and Coles 2019, 189).

These leaders also described this consistent training pattern. "We do teaching in different zones across North India. The training happens first in the zone office a few days a month, then the state office, then by areas, then by districts, then in subdistricts, then in villages. So everyone receives training" (163).

Is a Human Mediator Always Biblically Required for People to Be Effectively Taught by Scripture?

Most Protestants agree with the Westminster Confession of Faith (1.7) about the clear meaning of Scripture: "Those things which are necessary to be known, believed, and observed, for salvation, are so clearly explained in some part of Scripture that not only the learned, but the unlearned, using the usual means, can understand them well enough."

We believe God's Spirit can speak directly to his people by making Scripture clear. (This assumes access to a proper translation from the original languages.) Human teachers can help, but a human priesthood of intermediaries is not needed. The Reformers strongly supported this biblical idea against the claims of the Roman Catholic Church. Yet, in some cases, their modern followers have quietly set up their own approved intermediaries.

Misuse of biblical examples has overvalued ancient communication methods and discouraged using more repeatable ways of hearing from God's written word. For example, when Ezra went up his high wooden platform to teach God's people the Law (Neh 8:1–8), most people couldn't read, and written biblical text was rare. When the apostles did the teaching and preaching recorded in Acts, most people still couldn't read. Also, most of the New Testament had not yet been written, let alone compiled and made available to God's people individually. Mass printing of the Bible was 1,400 years away. Electronic distribution of Scripture was 1,900 years away. In biblical times, the best way to share God's truth with many people was one well-trained person talking to an audience.

Preaching as a structured speech still has value today. However, we now have repeatable ways to bring millions of people into direct personal contact with God's word. If we seriously intend to spread God's message to all the world's people, we need to use "all possible means" (1 Cor 9:22) to share the news of salvation. The goal of ongoing spiritual growth also calls us to prefer methods that don't make people depend on experts for spiritual feeding. The DBS approach used in many CPMs focuses on learning from and applying God's word. That word is alive and active to accomplish his purposes.

Scripture calls us toward making sure all people can hear and receive God's word. Limiting the messengers to only certain approved people is less important. Our first priority should be Spirit-led application of Scripture by as many people as possible. Interpretation by mature teachers is valuable. However, we should not make mature teachers a barrier, hindering the delivery of God's word to those who need to hear it.

What Is the Biblical Standard of Spiritual Maturity for Teaching Others?

Because of space limits, I suggest the two most basic texts: the criteria for elders found in 1 Timothy 3:2–7 and Titus 1:5–9. Titus 1:5 and Acts 14:21–23 describe finding local people who meet these criteria. This is the next step after the gospel first enters a group and part of building a mature church. The requirement, "He must not be a recent convert"

(1 Tim 3:6), applies, based on each local setting, as the gospel enters new groups and places.

When all local believers are fairly recent converts, this criterion takes a back seat to others. Philip Towner notes this in Paul's instruction to Titus for the Cretans: "Titus's task of appointing elders from among recent converts (notice that in this case Paul cannot rule out recent converts . . .) must not have been easy" (2010, 229). In CPMs, the local believers showing the most spiritual maturity are chosen for spiritual leadership.

What Do We Mean by Teaching?

Some of this second objection might come from CPM supporters' own use of the word *teach*. Trainers often say something like "outsiders help rather than teach." In that context, the intent is to avoid the common approach of "authoritatively explaining the meaning of a text." However, facilitating a DBS also counts as a form of nondirective biblical "teaching."

The Greek word *ginōskō* is used over two hundred times in the New Testament. It describes *learning through experience*, not just collecting facts. Teaching means "to cause a person to know something. . . . Teach, instruct, and train mean to cause to gain knowledge or skill. . . . Teach can be used for any way of passing on information or skill so that others may learn" (Merriam-Webster 2020).

How does this process happen? From our experience in classrooms and church, most of us think "teach" means a one-way lecture. One person talks and everyone else listens quietly and absorbs what they hear. But people learn in many ways, and one-way lectures turn out to be among the least effective—both for remembering and for changing lives. Much of the teaching in the New Testament was interactive. We see this in Jesus's interaction with his disciples and in the thirteen New Testament uses of the word *dialegomai* ("discuss, talk"). We find ten of *dialegomai*'s uses in Acts, describing Paul's way of proclaiming the message (17:2, 17; 18:4, 19; 19:8, 9).

CPMs use a variety of teaching methods. Many movements use inductive Bible study patterns. Some use more direct teaching, but in an interactive way. Most movements gather leaders in coaching groups for peer coaching and mutual learning. All have different levels of specific plans they use in discipleship.

Is There No Role for Teachers in CPM?

Yes, there is a role, but teachers need to impact everyday life, helping local people from start to finish. Our criteria for choosing teachers should be what most helps God's kingdom, not what most satisfies those who like to teach. We see in Scripture many descriptions and examples of teachers and teaching. CPMs aim to use this gift in the ways that will best produce mature, active, and growing disciples.

Objection 3

CPMs leave open a door for false teaching because of inadequate theological training for leaders.

This objection is based on two main ideas. First, how one defines adequate versus inadequate theological training. Second, the idea that the main or only way to prevent false teaching is theological training.

What is our standard for adequate theological training? For some Christians, the obvious answer would be an official degree from a recognized and biblically sound seminary. Or maybe at least a diploma or certificate from a recognized and biblically sound Bible school. Yet these traditional answers fall short in at least three important ways.

First, the Bible never mentions any of these criteria. That doesn't make them wrong answers, but it pushes us to think beyond our initial reaction if we want to find God's answer. Adequate training in the New Testament happened in different ways and settings. The modern academic model of training depends on many books and resources. The apostle Paul, by contrast, described his training model as easily repeatable to multiple generations: "And the things you have heard me say in the presence of many witnesses entrust to reliable people who will also be qualified to teach others" (2 Tim 2:2).

The criteria Paul listed for church leaders in 1 Timothy 3 included "able to teach," along with over a dozen other criteria. The qualities given to Titus include, "He must hold firmly to the trustworthy message as it has been taught, so that he can encourage others by sound doctrine and refute those who oppose it" (Titus 1:9).

These abilities can be developed in many ways, through interacting with mature teachers and God's word. The leaders of movements value biblical education, but they don't wait for disciples to finish a degree before preparing them to entrust God's truth to reliable people. And those reliable people, in turn, share the trustworthy message of the gospel with others too.

For example, Victor John says, "We also teach through everyday life lessons. Deuteronomy 6:7. . . . This teaching happens through being together in everyday life, not just sitting in a classroom" (John and Coles 2019, 161). He adds:

> Many ministries do a lot of theoretical training, with Bible college and so on, but they don't give people a chance to practice what they learn. We teach one thing then say, "Go and do it." So whatever they learn, they immediately apply in their lives. That's why they learn more. We teach a little, then they do it and learn from their experience as well as from our teaching. That helps them to really work effectively. When they learn from us, that starts the process. When they start doing what they learned, they learn many more things, because God is teaching them. (165)

CPMs aim for theology (knowledge of God's truth) to always lead to life application. Orthodoxy always connects to orthopraxy. Ott notes, "Church multiplication happens fastest where church planting does not need theologically trained and ordained pastors but is led by teams of regular or part-time workers . . . this is the New Testament pattern" (Ott and Wilson 2010, 385).

Second, most CPMs have a "pattern of sound teaching" passed on to believers in the movement. Disciples are eager to study the Bible. This often leads to the development of increasingly strong natural theological training. For example, Shodankeh Johnson (2021) describes how the training process in their CPM in Sierra Leone grew into a four-year college. It started as a Bible study in 1998, which grew into a one-year certificate course. Within a few years, the government approved the course curriculum for four-year degrees. The school now offers four-year degrees in theology and many other fields. Extended biblical training plays an important role in many CPMs.

Third, a quick look shows that theological education does not always stop false teaching. For example, I was raised in a Protestant church with many sad tales. I heard stories of (and sermons from) pastors whose faith was less biblically sound *after* seminary than before. Theological knowledge can be useful, but it doesn't ensure the ability to build healthy biblical faith in others. Many modern heresies come from theologians with doctorates from seminaries. Heretical movements often start with a talented teacher. The person's teaching is so impressive that their followers tend to uncritically accept and repeat whatever they say. Notable examples include Jehovah's Witnesses, Christian Science, and Mormonism. Many heretical groups in the past have been named after the gifted teacher who effectively taught wrong interpretations. Examples include Apollinarism, Arianism, Sabellianism, Marcionism, Montanism, Henricians, and Pelagianism.

The leaders of movements build strong biblical faith through interactive study and application of God's word. Every disciple is trained to work with Scripture and apply it for themselves. They are also trained to ask each other, "Where do you see that in the Bible?" This is one of the best ways to prevent heresy. Movement leaders also usually have some connection with the global and historical body of Christ. This allows comparison and safety in the movement's interpretation and application of Scripture.

Disciples in CPMs consistently apply the "one another" commands of Scripture. This provides mutual accountability in the way of the Lord and helps avoid false teaching. They regularly practice living out verses such as the following: "Let the message of Christ dwell among you richly as you teach and admonish one another" (Col 3:16). "Therefore encourage each other and build each other up, just as in fact you are doing" (1 Thess 5:11). "But encourage each other daily, as long as it is called 'Today,' so that none of you may become hardened by sin's deceitfulness" (Heb 3:13).

Many Christian leaders think that correct preaching results in correct theology in the listeners. Studies, however, show that this is false (Weber 2018). Listeners in the pew never have to deal with their wrong theology. In CPMs, believers struggle with God's word at a deeper level than just hearing it. In small group Bible discussions, issues tend to come out more quickly. People either grow in holiness or leave. One research project concluded: "No significant patterns of heresy were found among those dozen movements" (Sergeant 2019, Loc 2730–41).

In the fallen world of this age, God's people will always face the temptation of false teaching. No amount or type of theological training can "error-proof" God's people. We see in the New Testament that even the best teaching didn't stop all false teaching. Paul's approach included his "pattern of sound teaching" (2 Tim 1:13; cf. Rom 6:17). It also involved ongoing relationships, through letters, to address various issues as they arose. And

Paul relied heavily on local pastoral leaders guarding the flock (cf. Acts 20:28–31; Titus 1:9). Leaders of movements often use similar prevention methods to guard against false teaching.

Objection 4

CPMs have inadequate ecclesiology. (Their "churches" may not be real churches.)

Interestingly, Ott and Wilson write,

> Many of the churches planted by Paul would not meet what many today might consider a minimal standard for being an established church. Nevertheless, he addressed even the most problematical congregations as "the church." This makes us think more carefully about what really makes a local church in the biblical sense. (2010, 4)

This objection that "their 'churches' may not be real churches" shows a lack of accurate information about the reality among CPMs. The concern seems to be based on one or more of three things:

1. Lack of information about actual CPMs
2. Criteria for "church" too dependent on Western church traditions
3. Confusion of CPMs with "Insider Movements," many of which do, in my opinion, have inadequate ecclesiology[9]

A pattern used by many movements is known as "church circles" (Smith 2012, 22-26). This tool helps leaders track the growth and maturing of groups into churches. It uses the biblical descriptions in Acts 2:36–47 and other New Testament texts. These circles usually include baptism, God's word, the Lord's Supper, fellowship, giving and ministry, prayer, praise, evangelism, and leadership.

Throughout the New Testament, Jesus's followers mainly gathered for worship in homes. Believers also followed this pattern during the first two hundred years of church history. This gathering pattern is no longer the most common. However, hopefully no one (directly or indirectly) sees house churches as "not real churches."

---

9 See Waterman's critique of Insider Movement ecclesiology and features of biblical *ekklēsia* (Waterman 2011, 460–67; Waterman 2016).

A survey of various criteria or signs of the church has found only one major "sign" that some might argue is missing in CPMs. For example, the Belgic Confession, written in 1561, lists the "marks by which the true Church is known." The first mark is "If the pure doctrine of the gospel is preached therein" (Belgic Confession n.d.).

This could give critics a reason to exclude CPM patterns from their view of churches. One could interpret "preached" to mean an ordained male pastor standing behind a pulpit, giving a one-way message to a passive group of laypeople. This would have been the intent of those who wrote the Belgic Confession. We can ask whether modern critics use this criterion when they accuse CPMs of weak ecclesiology. They might say CPMs don't have "preaching" of the word. They have no pulpit, no expert on a stage giving a long speech, and no passive listeners.

The presentation of God's word in CPMs often follows a different pattern. Sometimes a leader may explain biblical truth to a mostly silent group. However, deeper engagement with Scripture usually happens in an interactive way, as in a DBS. Everyone gets actively involved in thinking, discussing, and applying the truths of Scripture. They likely don't have a pulpit. And they don't think one person has all the right answers. They focus on applying God's word, often with clear accountability to each other for obeying what they have learned.

Movements prefer to have disciples who always apply God's word rather than passive listeners to weekly polished speeches. But I suspect that the absence of weekly Sunday "preaching" makes some people think the disciples' gatherings in CPMs are not "real churches."

One version of this objection can be found in the article "9 Marks of a Healthy Church" (9Marks n.d.). The first mark ("Preaching") states, "An expositional sermon takes the main point of a passage of Scripture, makes it the main point of the sermon, and applies it to life today."

I personally prefer expository sermons over other preaching styles. If this definition of preaching were seen as the *only* proper way to present Scripture to God's people, it would exclude most CPMs. But it would also exclude most *other* churches (including evangelical churches) worldwide. I suspect topical sermons far outnumber expository sermons—both globally and historically. God intends for his word to be understood and applied in his children's lives. We do better to focus on accomplishing that goal rather than demanding one specific and limited way to reach that goal.

One respondent to my survey regarding these eight objections wrote:

> Serious Bible students . . . would probably ask if the traits of the early church seen in Acts 2 and Acts 4 and Paul's many commands to one another are happening in a given movement. And surely the answer they would find is yes. Then they would ask if there were elders, and find the answer is yes. And they would ask about a good understanding of the truth, and the answer would be yes. Then they would ask if they are building unity with other parts of the body of Christ, and the answer would be yes—yes, that is, where enough time on each of these has allowed development of them, I would estimate one to two years sometimes.

As noted by this respondent, the process of groups becoming churches takes some time. Yet each CPM has an idea of what they consider to be a church (*ekklēsia*). And they use criteria generally consistent with the characteristics found in the New Testament (Waterman 2011).

Objection 5

The "Person of Peace" strategy is not really taught in Matthew, Luke, or Acts.

Some supporters of CPM have presented more details for the "person of peace" strategy than we find clearly taught in the New Testament texts. We can see this in the slightly different descriptions of a person of peace given by different CPM trainers. However, we can see in the New Testament a clear pattern the apostles often used when entering new places. When Jesus sent out the Twelve, he told them: "Look for some worthy person and stay at their house until you leave" (Matt 10:11).

New Testament scholar D. A. Carson, in his commentary on Matthew, says of this sending, "It is surely not unnatural for Jesus to treat this mission of the Twelve as both a clear short-term plan and a model for the longer mission in the years ahead. The Twelve become a model for other disciples in their witness after Pentecost" (1984, 242).

We see a similar instruction in Jesus's sending of the seventy-two in Luke 10. "Whatever house you enter, first say, 'Peace be to this house!' And if a son of peace is there, your peace will rest upon him. But if not, it will return to you. And remain in the same house . . ." (Luke 10:5–7 ESV). This pattern shows up again in many stories in Acts as well. For example,

Cornelius (Acts 10), Lydia (16:14–15), and the Philippian jailer (16:31–32). Over and over, an openhearted person of influence opens the doors to bring their family into faith in Christ.

The New Testament does not show this as the only way to reach people in a new area. However, it does show this approach both in divine command and apostolic example. Throughout church history, God has used key people to open doors effectively for the gospel to those within their sphere of influence. Thousands of everyday examples are lost in history. Yet we have records of many key people whose conversions led their sphere of influence toward Christ. This would include Ezana of Axum (northern Ethiopia and parts of four other nations in the fourth century), Mirian III of Iberia, Sigeberht of East Anglia, Peada of Mercia, Olof Skötkonung (king of Sweden), Ranavalona II (queen of Madagascar), and Pōmare II (king of Tahiti).

At present, movements are growing most rapidly in the Majority World. God is using this growth to remind Westerners of a biblical truth. People from non-Christian backgrounds don't always come to faith as isolated individuals, standing against everyone else they know. People often come to faith with family members or important others who connect with their faith journey. We see this in New Testament descriptions, in the frequent use of the word *oikos*. We also see it in Majority World settings of the twenty-first century. The most notable exception to this common global pattern of faith journeys is Western culture in recent centuries.

Sadly, this individualistic exception seems to underlie the experience and preference of most critics of CPM. We don't gain anything by arguing about details of the description of a person of peace. We also shouldn't say that finding a person of peace is the only right way to start new work in an unreached place or group. However, we see the important role of a "key person" in Jesus's teaching and the examples in Acts. We see it also in historical and current evidence of major gospel advance. So, it seems unhelpful to object to movement leaders being trained and encouraged to look for a person of peace in new locations.

Objection 6

Obedience-based discipleship is a dangerous paradigm. It runs the risk of bypassing grace and teaching legalism.

If "obedience-based discipleship" meant trying to earn salvation through obedience, that would be bad. However, the phrase is meant to simply reflect one basic part of Jesus's command to "make disciples." He said, "teaching them to obey everything I have commanded you" (Matt 28:19–20). Warrick Farah comments:

> Much of today's forms of discipleship are based on a Western education model of church, where people were seen as lacking the right doctrine and theology. This is certainly important, but it is also incomplete. Jesus' focus in Matthew 28 seems to put the emphasis on behavior. Learning to do all that Jesus "has commanded" necessarily includes a biblical view of life, where word and deed, plus the spiritual and the social, are combined into one clear unity. (2020, 6)

CPMs often build a foundation for faith through a chronological study of "creation to Christ" passages. This copies (in brief form) the pattern God used through thousands of years of Old Testament history. We know that "God . . . announced the gospel in advance to Abraham" (Gal 3:8) and that God's grace received by faith underpinned the law (Gen 15:6; Exod 19:4–8). Also, "the law was our guardian until Christ came that we might be justified by faith" (Gal 3:24). New Testament proclamation of the gospel was built solidly on centuries of calls for obedience. God spent thousands of years calling people to obedience before giving a clear revelation of salvation through Christ.

Taking a few weeks (or months) for a brief chronological study through creation to Christ passages builds a basic understanding of essential truths. These include the true nature of God and of sin, the need for the blood sacrifice to forgive sin, and the promise of a redeeming sacrifice. I hope we all see it as positive when any person reads the Bible and tries to obey God based on what they have read. Of course, only the power of the Holy Spirit makes God-pleasing obedience possible. An unbeliever's attempts at obedience can never earn salvation.

Yet, from a biblical view, it seems good if people learn from the start that the right response to God's word is to apply its teaching. This differs greatly from the too-common pattern in some churches. Many Christians act as if the right response to God's word is just to analyze, explain, and understand it intellectually. Accurate understanding is valuable when it leads to obedience. But as an end in itself, it falls far short of the discipleship to which Jesus calls us.

The phrase "obedience-based discipleship" is never presented as a replacement for "grace-based discipleship" or "love-based discipleship." In fact, David and Paul Watson explain Jesus's teaching on the essential link between love and obedience (Watson and Watson 2014, 39–45). They note a clear relationship: "If you love me, you will obey what I command" (John 14:15). They also discuss Jesus's explanation of this theme in John 14:16–25 and John's repetition of it in 1 John 5:3–4. However, I disagree with the Watsons' unclear wording: "Jesus equated 'obedience' to 'love' in the Gospel of John" (39). I would clarify that Jesus showed obedience as a *result* of love, not the same as it. The Watsons themselves show this more accurate connection a few pages later. They explain: "Our motives for being obedient determine if we are doing so out of love or legalism" (45).

The phrase "obedience-based discipleship" is meant to highlight a contrast between two kinds of "discipleship." Does it consist of active obedience or just knowing or agreeing with right beliefs? Christians too often treat religious knowledge as an end in itself. God clearly intends that greater knowledge of his truth should always lead to greater obedience. Scripture gives a strong warning that just adding knowledge risks *increasing* sin! "If anyone, then, knows the good they ought to do and doesn't do it, it is sin for them" (Jas 4:17). For this reason, DMMs stress the importance of obedience in discipleship, not just knowledge.

Does obedience-based discipleship skip grace and teach legalism? This concern does not seem to come from any research among DMMs. I've never heard or seen any evidence of DMM disciples trying to be justified by obeying laws. Neither have I seen evidence of DMMs failing to teach salvation by grace through faith. In fact, the story sets chosen for DBS emphasize that we cannot please God by obeying the law. We need a Savior. One sample set of DBS stories includes these clear lessons on commitment and discipleship:

- Who is Jesus? John 1:1–18
- What does Jesus offer you and ask you? John 14:1–7, 23–27
- What is the result of faith in Jesus? John 3:3–21
- What is your response? Acts 2:36–41; Psalm 32:1–5; Romans 10:9–10
- What is baptism? Romans 6:1–4; Galatians 3:26–28; Acts 10:44–48

Objections seem to come mainly from two concerns. First, the truth that God's grace, rather than obedience, must be the basis of discipleship (e.g., Pratt 2015, 9–10). For this reason, I agree that the wording "obedience-based discipleship" is not ideal. It aims to show the importance of obedience rather than *just* knowledge. However, it has unintentionally led some people to think of an idea never intended: obedience as the foundation of discipleship. It seems this concern has come from unclear wording of the idea rather than a real problem among CPMs.

Second, objections have arisen to calling for obedience before presenting the gospel of grace (e.g., Kocman 2019). This concern seems to have been made worse by using the phrase "disciple people to conversion" (Trousdale 2012, 43). This wording is based on Jesus's years of interaction with his disciples before they knew of his divine nature or his death for their sins. However, to talk about "discipling" unbelievers can cause misunderstanding. In fact a person cannot be Jesus's disciple until they know about Jesus and decide to follow him. For that reason, I prefer to avoid the confusing phrase "disciple to conversion." I do, however, agree with DMM's Bible-based process leading toward commitment.

The main point is that, for most people, coming to saving faith involves a process. It is almost never just a momentary decision. The process is especially important for those without prior biblical knowledge or background. We need to consider what that process must include to bring a person to saving faith. One essential ingredient is the work of God's Spirit drawing the person (John 6:44). And certainly also God's word: "Consequently, faith comes from hearing the message, and the message is heard through the word about Christ" (Rom 10:17).

So we ask, "Do we want unbelievers to hear and think about God's word?" Yes! And when a not-yet-believer hears and thinks about God's word, what response do we hope for? Do we hope for just passive listening until God's Spirit finishes drawing the person and they make a faith commitment? Or do we hope that God's word inspires some life response even during the process?

A creation to Christ DBS never promises salvation based on applying God's word before faith in Christ. The issue of justification starts to be addressed when a chronological overview of salvation history reaches that point. Westerners who came to faith from a Christian-context background need to realize an important fact. A process is usually required for those from a non-Christian background to come to saving faith. To the extent we recognize the need for a process, we become less worried about the steps involved. We make provision for each person or group to gradually grow in understanding of the foundations of saving grace. Each step plays a part in leading to salvation by faith in the person and work of Jesus Christ.

For some people, the phrase "obedience-based discipleship" has become a stumbling block. So, I prefer the phrase "obedience-normal discipleship," highlighting this wonderful trait of CPMs. Believers see obedience as normal. It's just the obvious thing people do when they love and follow Jesus as their Lord. It's not obedience instead of grace as the foundation of discipleship. It's obedience to God's word instead of just knowing God's word as the normal pattern of discipleship.

Objection 7

Discovery Bible Study (DBS) is not a biblical approach to evangelism. The biblical pattern is proclamation.

This objection contains a false choice. The leader of a movement in SE Asia said,

> The biblical pattern is proclamation, as understood in the biblical context. Many of the examples we see in the Bible are not large groups (we tend to think of proclamation as for large groups), but there are more discussions with small groups of people, some of which start as talks with individuals, than there are large-group proclamations.
>
> The fact that we focus on DBS does not mean we don't do the proclamation we do in large groups. . . . This is very common, but is a different strategy outside the DBS groups. . . .

The fact that we focus on DBS does not mean we don't do the Transformation Dialogs we do before and building up to DBS groups. These may start with individuals, but we try to move them into talks in groups about spiritual truth, and this leads to DBS gatherings.

In other words, the New Testament shows proclamation happening in many ways and settings. And in modern movements, proclamation can and does happen in many ways. DBS is just one approach. If by "not biblical," one means "not clearly mentioned in the Bible," the same accusation would apply to many practices common among Christians. It would apply, for example, to altar calls, tracts, Bible distribution, radio, TV, satellite broadcasts, the *Jesus* film, and specific church buildings. The accusation would land much wider than probably any critic intends.

If by "not biblical" one means "against biblical teaching," this objection becomes just another way of stating the following concern.

Objection 8

It is unwise and dangerous to have unbelievers studying the Bible without any mature Christian present to guide their study.

The first response to this concern must be to refer to what has already been said about the clear meaning of Scripture. This objection assumes a human intermediary is needed for accurate communication of God's message. This seems based on the wrong idea that God's word and God's Spirit are not enough to present God's truth.

Jesus, by contrast, spoke well of people being taught directly by God as a way to saving faith. "It is written in the Prophets: 'They will all be taught by God.' Everyone who has heard the Father and learned from him comes to me" (John 6:45). A main way the Father draws not-yet-believers to Jesus is for them to listen to and follow God's word. Merrill Tenney comments, "Verse 45 shows that God would do his drawing through Scriptures and that those who obey God's will as shown in the Scriptures would come to Jesus" (1981, 76).

D. A. Carson comments on this verse, "Jesus in the Farewell Discourse promises the coming of the Holy Spirit—with a teaching role (14:26–27; 16:12–15)" (1991, 293). And the Pulpit Commentary states, "Direct teaching by God is the main requirement of any spiritual understanding, even of the mysteries of Christ the Revealer. . . . Divine teaching by the Spirit of the Father and Son is the first step . . . to believing in Christ" (Exell and Spence 1950, 265).

This objection shows too little trust in God's ability to speak through his word and his Spirit. It also shows too much trust in human teachers and our ability to accurately share God's truth. It also reflects a misunderstanding about the DBS process. Maybe the usual role of a more mature believer in the DBS process has not always been clearly explained. Unbelievers are not left completely alone with no guidance in their study of Scripture. Usually, a more mature believer plays some role in the group's interaction with Scripture.

This is seen first in the choice of recommended texts to study (such as a creation to Christ sequence or texts relevant to a specific need of the group). It is then usually seen in the regular mentoring (shadow pastoring) of one or two members of the group. In most cases, the believer meets regularly with this person(s) to discuss the next text to be studied. They also respond to any concerns or questions that have come up from the previous study. In this way, the group's journey to faith is guided by someone more mature in the faith. At the same time, group members themselves can wrestle with how to understand and apply biblical truths in their unique context. This process trusts the Holy Spirit to "guide them into all truth."

Conclusions and Recommendations

Having discussed all eight of the most common types of objections to CPMs, I offer a few conclusions and recommendations.

1. Many problems blamed on CPMs have been based on hearsay or on looking at ministries that do not actually fit the criteria of a CPM.[10] In some cases, accusations have been multiplied by wrongly grouping CPM/DMM together with Insider Movements or other non-CPM approaches. Here is one example: "The overemphasis on speed and practicality in the Church Planting Movement, Disciple-Making Movement, Insider Movement, Short-Cycle Church Planting, and similar is a dangerous result of bad theology" (Buser and Vegas 2020).

---

10 Defined as consistent, multiple-stream, fourth-generation reproduction of local churches.

2. Many objections to CPMs come from a lack of information about what actually happens in CPMs. In many cases, those involved in CPMs have been hesitant to share much information with the wider world. They have wanted to avoid having overzealous Christians or hostile non-Christians rush in and harm the ministry. More complete information about some movements has recently become more widely available.[11] More study is needed, and we should all stay open to learn more about what is and isn't happening in CPMs.

3. Some objections come from assumptions based on traditional church patterns in Christendom. We don't need to argue against or insult traditional patterns. However, we do well to notice differences between what Scripture actually says and what we have thought it says or patterns chosen as Western applications. CPMs invite us to see with fresh eyes the simplicity of the gospel message. They invite us to notice repeatable patterns that allowed the gospel to spread rapidly in early centuries. And they call us to believe for similar growth in many places today.

4. The wording of some CPM supporters and trainers has sometimes been less than careful. In some cases, CPM trainings have included weak biblical interpretation or left room for misunderstandings. In other cases, overzealous promotion of CPM has led to inaccurate descriptions of movements or disrespect toward traditional church and church planting models. However, inaccurate or unhelpful statements by proponents do not cancel out a confirmed reality. Millions of unbelievers are becoming disciples of Christ in over two thousand known CPMs globally.

God's kingdom is growing greatly through CPMs and DMMs today. We see this growth most clearly among many least reached groups. CPMs are reaching groups that have mostly remained untouched by past centuries of mission outreach. In many places, the harvest field is becoming a harvest force. Obedient disciples are making more disciples, and local churches are starting new churches. Movements are often misunderstood, but we

---

11 Examples of in-depth case studies of movements include Garrison 2014, Reach 2016, Larsen and a Fruitful Band of Brothers 2018, John and Coles 2019, Coles and Parks 2019, Larsen and Focus on Fruit Team 2020, Farah 2021, Tasse and Coles 2024, B. R. and Coles 2025, and Dubois, Parks, and Long 2025.

can find great encouragement in these apparent works of God. When we compare the realities of modern CPMs to the commands and examples of Scripture, we can see the family resemblance. We look forward to seeing how these movements will endure and manifest God's kingdom in the years to come.

References

9Marks. n.d. "9 Marks of a Healthy Church," 9Marks, www.9marks.org/about/the-nine-marks.

Belgic Confession. n.d. "Belgic Confession." Christian Reformed Church. https://www.crcna.org/welcome/beliefs/confessions/belgic-confession.

B. R., Aychi, with Dave Coles. 2025. *Living Fire: Advancing God's Kingdom in Challenging Places*. BEYOND & Experience Life.

Buser, Brooks, and Chad Vegas. 2020. "Why Unreached People Groups Still Matter in Missions." The Gospel Coalition, January 10, 2020, https://www.thegospelcoalition.org/article/why-unreached-people-groups-still-matter-in-missions/.

Carson, D. A. 1984. "Matthew." In *The Expositor's Bible Commentary*, Vol. 8. Zondervan.

Carson, D. A. 1991. *The Gospel According to John*. Eerdmans.

Coles, Dave, and Stan Parks. 2019. *24:14—A Testimony to All Peoples*. 24:14.

Dubois, William, Stan Parks, Justin Long. 2025. *Forests in the Seed: How Kingdom Movements Are Multiplying Across the Unreached World*. Patmos Education Group.

Exell, Joseph, and H. D. M. Spence, eds. 1950. *The Pulpit Commentary*. 23 vols. https://biblehub.com/commentaries/pulpit/john/6.htm.

Farah, Warrick. 2020. "Motus Dei: Disciple-Making Movements and the Mission of God." *Global Missiology* 2, no. 17.

Farah, Warrick. 2021. *Motus Dei: The Movement of God to Disciple the Nations*. William Carey Publishing.

Garrison, David. 2014. *A Wind in the House of Islam: How God Is Drawing Muslims Around the World to Faith in Jesus Christ*. WIGTake Resources.

John, Victor, with Dave Coles. 2019. *Bhojpuri Breakthrough: A Movement That Keeps Multiplying*. WIGTake Resources.

Johnson, Shodankeh. 2021. *Same God Here!* Moody.

Kocman, Alex. 2019. "Is 'Obedience-Based Discipleship' Biblical?" https://www.abwe.org/blog/obedience-based-discipleship-biblical.

Larsen, Trevor, and a Fruitful Band of Brothers. 2018. *Focus on Fruit! Movement Case Studies & Fruitful Practices*. Indonesia.

Larsen, Trevor, and Focus on Fruit Team. 2020. *Core Skills of Movement Leaders: Repeating Patterns from Generation to Generation.*

Ott, Craig, and Gene Wilson. 2010. *Global Church Planting.* Baker Academic.

Pratt, Zane. 2015. "Obedience-Based Discipleship." *Global Missiology.*

Reach, Robert. 2016. *Movements That Move: 7 Root Principles That Nurture Church Planting Movements.* ChurchSmart Resources.

Sergeant, Curtis. 2019. *The Only One.* William Carey Publishing.

Smith, Steve. 2012. "The Bare Essentials of Helping Groups Become Churches: Four Helps in CPM." *Mission Frontiers* (September-October 2012).

Tasse, Aila, with Dave Coles. 2024. *Cabbages in the Desert: How God Transformed a Devout Muslim and Catalyzed Disciple Making Movements Among Unreached Peoples.* Beyond.

Tenney, Merrill. 1981. "The Gospel of John." In *The Expositor's Bible Commentary*, Vol. 9. Zondervan.

Throckmorton, Warren. 2020. "Gospel for Asia Invades Africa." www.wthrockmorton.com/category/k-p-yohannan.

Towner, Philip. 2010. *1–2 Timothy and Titus.* IVP Academic.

Trousdale, Jerry. 2012. *Miraculous Movements.* Thomas Nelson.

Waterman, L. D. 2011. "What Is Church? From Surveying Scripture to Applying in Culture." *Evangelical Missions Quarterly* 47, no. 4.

Waterman, L. D. 2016. "A Book Review of Understanding Insider Movements." https://btdnetwork.org/wp-content/uploads/Blogs/2016/Review%20-%20Understanding%20Insider%20Movements.pdf.

Watson, David, and Paul Watson. 2014. *Contagious Disciple Making.* Thomas Nelson.

Weber, Jeremy. 2018. "Christian, What Do You Believe? Probably a Heresy About Jesus, Says Survey." *Christianity Today*, October 16, 2018. https://www.christianitytoday.com/news/2018/october/what-do-christians-believe-ligonier-state-theology-heresy.html.

Westminster Confession of Faith. bpc.org/wp-content/uploads/2015/06/D-ConfessionOfFaith.pdf.

Zylstra, Sarah. 2019. "Gospel for Asia Settles Lawsuit with $37 Million Refund to Donors." *Christianity Today*, March 01, 2019. www.christianitytoday.com/news/2019/march/gospel-for-asia-gfa-settles-class-action-refund-donors.html.

WILLIAM CAREY PUBLISHING
Available at missionbooks.org

Motus Dei:
The Movement of God to Disciple the Nations

Warrick Farah, editor

This book offers over thirty first-hand accounts of indigenous churches planting churches among the nation. The resulting in-depth analysis of movements provides a multi-disciplinary academic investigation of an emerging "movements missiology." *Motus Dei* locates the current church planting movement (CPM) phenomenon within modern history, while tracing its roots back to the first century, and articulates a missiological description of the dynamics of Disciple Making Movements (DMMs).

Mobilizing Movements: Leadership Insights for Discipling Whole Nations

Murray Moerman

Moerman provides realistic expectations of what it takes to facilitate a movement and how to gain the support of various partners needed for long-term success, resulting in whole-nation church planting saturation. Based on years of research, *Mobilizing Movements* contains both practical and spiritual elements. You will find insights and models from several continents for macro (whole nation) strategies and micro (personal) disciple-making.

WILLIAM CAREY PUBLISHING
Available at missionbooks.org

Fruit to Harvest: Witness of God's Great Work among Muslims

Gene Daniels, Pam Arlund, and Jim Haney, editors

This book is a cultural anthology written by a diverse group of gospel workers who live with and love Muslims. You will join a global mission conversation at the forefront of gospel advance—the world of Islam. Like its predecessor (*From Seed to Fruit*), this book is the result of a global consultation sponsored by the Vision 5:9 Network—insights from hundreds of testimonies are taken from field workers in thirty different agencies working across the Muslim world.

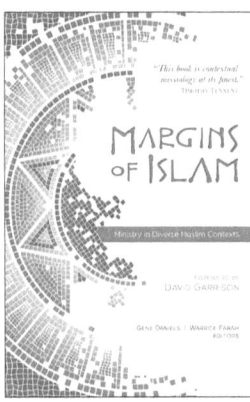

Margins of Islam: Ministry in Diverse Muslim Contexts

Gene Daniels and Warrick Farah, editors

What do you do when "Islam" does not adequately describe the Muslims you know? *Margins of Islam* brings together scholar-practitioners who explain their own approaches to a diversity of Muslims across the world. Each chapter grapples with a context that is significantly different from the way Islam is traditionally presented in mission texts. These crucial differences may be theological, socio-political, ethnic, or a specific variation of Islam in a context—but they all shape the way we do mission.

www.ingramcontent.com/pod-product-compliance
Lightning Source LLC
Chambersburg PA
CBHW060613080526
44585CB00013B/812